ALSO BY TRACY McCUBBIN

Making Space, Clutter Free:
The Last Book on Decluttering
You'll Ever Need

make

space

for

Happiness

How to Stop Attracting Clutter and Start Magnetizing the Life You Want

tracy mccubbin

 sourcebooks

Published by Sourcebooks
P.O. Box 4410, Naperville, Illinois 60567-4410
(630) 961-3900
sourcebooks.com

Library of Congress Cataloging-in-Publication Data

Names: McCubbin, Tracy, author.
Title: Make space for happiness : how to stop attracting clutter and start magnetizing the life you want / Tracy McCubbin.
Description: Naperville, Illinois : Sourcebooks, [2022]
Identifiers: LCCN 2022006670 (print) | LCCN 2022006671 (ebook) | (trade paperback) | (epub)
Subjects: LCSH: Simplicity. | Orderliness.
Classification: LCC BJ1496 .M385 2022 (print) | LCC BJ1496 (ebook) | DDC 179/.9--dc23/eng/20220511
LC record available at https://lccn.loc.gov/2022006670
LC ebook record available at https://lccn.loc.gov/2022006671

Printed and bound in the United States of America.
VP 10 9 8 7 6 5 4 3 2 1

For Rich.
Thank you for filling up my life with love.

contents

INTRODUCTION   1

1. your 7 emotional clutter magnets   13

2. magnetize true connection   39

3. magnetize strong self-confidence   65

4. magnetize free time   85

5. magnetize big love   109

6. magnetize self-respect   133

7. magnetize your real purpose   151

8. magnetize lasting wisdom   177

CONCLUSION: *you are enough*   193

APPENDIX: *adverse childhood experience (ace)*

   questionnaire   199

ENDNOTES   203

INDEX   208

ACKNOWLEDGMENTS   212

ABOUT THE AUTHOR   215

INTRODUCTION

GLOBALLY, 2020 WAS A CRUCIBLE FOR MANY people—and for many reasons. For those of us who were fortunate enough to keep our health, we still faced enormous upheaval as we moved our lives indoors and hunkered down. A home that had served as little more than a changing room before the pandemic suddenly became a person's entire world. In my role as a professional organizer and declutterer, I saw my clients in Los Angeles and across the country have a reckoning with their home environments unlike anything we have ever experienced in our lifetime.

My assessment: we are in crisis. A stuff crisis.

Whenever I had the occasion to get in my car and quickly zip across Los Angeles during lockdown, I couldn't help but notice that most of the vehicles on the street were UPS, DHL, FedEx, and Amazon. So many Amazon trucks. So many, in fact, that I started to notice that unmarked vans had slapped on Amazon magnets and drivers in orange vests were popping out of them with armloads of packages. Then I started to notice the piles of packages on doorsteps. Piles. Every front stoop looked like a Leaning Tower of Packages. Blue recycle bins were barfing out empty cardboard boxes. When I finally started to work in clients' homes again, I was shocked at the amount of shopping they had done. It looked as if they had rebought everything they had decluttered before—and then some.

For many people, having to be stuck at home confronting their disorder, disarray, and excess, was a rough awakening. Previously, they could hunt down their keys, or their "good" blouse, or the "right" travel mug, and eventually get out the door. They could promise themselves once again that they would deal with their clutter "soon." But during the pandemic, they had nothing to do but accept that their homes had become unmanageable. Just like overeating or drinking too much, overshopping is fun in the moment but there is always a heavy price to pay later.

I thought business for dClutterfly[1] would be slow as lockdown restrictions lifted. Instead, I ended up hiring more employees to help me get my clients' clutter under control so that bedrooms, garages, and kitchen counters could become offices, so that children could go to school from home, and so that families who used to sit down for a meal once a week could now eat three meals a day together and work alongside one another with minimal friction. And that's not to mention helping all the people moving. Aging parents moving in with their adult children to stay safe and help with the grandkids. Grown adults moving back in with their parents due to the economic downturn. People deciding it was time to get out of the city and move somewhere quieter. Everyone trying to make big shifts happen quickly was confronted with how much stuff they had and how little they needed.

What did "helping" mean?

In some instances, we emptied garages of broken lawn mowers and unused furniture. There was gently used baby gear to pass along. We helped consolidate closets so that one could be converted to an office. We packed up china from credenzas and replaced it with school supplies.

But, primarily, what people called us for was to deal with the overwhelming *excess*. The hallway lined with boxes. The closet filled with untouched shopping bags. The kitchen drawers bursting with multiple unused gadgets. The den filled with dusty exercise equipment.

Look, we all need things. I own many, many things. I have things I cook with, things I bathe with, things I wear, and things I work with. I even have things I just like to look at because they make me happy.

But when we have *excessive* amounts—more than our homes can hold, more than we can clean and care for, more than we can ever use—we need to reflect. After being home twenty-four hours a day for months on end, we have to ask ourselves how much do we really use? How much stuff do we really need?

Let's agree that if we weren't dusting off the treadmill during the pandemic, we are never going to.

Despite everything advertisers want us to believe, stuff does not make us healthy or better or more successful. It doesn't give us longevity, and it certainly doesn't help the planet. *Most* importantly, it is scientifically proven that stuff does not make us happy.

And your happiness is what I care about.

I grew up in California, the daughter of a wonderful man with an intractable hoarding problem, so I saw firsthand the tenacious pull that stuff can have on our psyches. As an adult in Los Angeles, I became a personal assistant known for being able to tackle any organizational challenge. As word spread, my business was born, and dClutterfly is now Los Angeles's premier home organization company.

Over many years and after seeing thousands of homes, I started to recognize patterns. Clutter that people couldn't let go of stood directly between how they were living and how they *wanted* to be living. In my last book, *Making Space, Clutter Free*, I introduced people to the concept of Emotional Clutter Blocks. My seven Clutter Blocks are the mind traps we can easily get stuck in when we're unable to let go of possessions that we don't want, use, or love. Let me explain more.

Clutter Block #1: *My Stuff Keeps Me in the Past* runs us when we hold on tightly to things like old trophies, gifts from exes, and sympathy cards from past acquaintances. This is unhelpful because it signals that our best days are behind us.

Clutter Block #2: *My Stuff Tells Me Who I Am* tells us to hang on to clothes and accessories that we don't wear but keep because of the designer label. The clutter keeps us company, and we hold onto the labels and brands that give us false status.

Clutter Block #3: *The Stuff I'm Avoiding* is usually the administrative detritus that people allow to pile up rather than dispatch. Notices from the IRS, unsigned power of attorney forms, documents that just need a good shredder;

being a grown-up means facing the thing and dealing with it.

Clutter Block #4: *My Fantasy Stuff for My Fantasy Life* blocks against letting go of stuff we buy to magically think ourselves into the life we think we should be living. It could be anticipatory maternity clothes, suits for a job we haven't applied for, or the sport we are somehow going to take up.

Clutter Block #5: *I'm Not Worth My Good Stuff* stops us from using wedding presents, tag-laden evening wear, or the "good" candles and "nice" soaps that sit waiting for a special day that may never come.

Clutter Block #6: *Trapped with Other People's Stuff* sticks people with inherited clothes and furniture they don't like, never wanted, and cannot release because it feels disrespectful to those who have passed.

And last, Clutter Block #7: *The Stuff I Keep Paying For* keeps us from setting free a purchase mistake. We hold on to something we don't need, want, or use because we "paid a lot" for it. This leads to a compounded mistake of paying for storage or turning rooms in our home into storage depots. There is a reason why storage is a billion-dollar industry—and yet almost nothing in those units is worth the cost of storing them.

What we found was that when we focused on healing the underlying emotional need, my clients and my readers were suddenly able to let go of stuff that had plagued them for years. Best of all, they were able to start living the way they had always wanted to before their stuff got in the way.

At the end of the day, it's how you live that I care the most about. Not rainbow-sorting your shoes or decanting all your beans. I want your keys where you can grab 'em, permission slips in an outbox, and your vegetable peeler visible when you open the drawer. I want your home to be a tool that enables you to *do* the things you want to do, like get ready for work, spend time with your family, or relax. I certainly don't want you to constantly confront piles of stuff that make you feel bad.

Making Space, Clutter Free came out in 2019, and soon after, my inbox and Instagram were flooded with pictures of once-cluttered homes transformed into decluttered, useful spaces that set people up to be living the lives they wanted.

But then...I noticed something new. Some of my clients and followers healed their blocks and released their excess stuff. And then, they kept buying.

I started to think back over my Mavens of Multiples, or clients and community members who acquire excess in one or two categories. For example, wellness products on recurring subscriptions. Or more pantry staples than anyone will ever need—even during a pandemic or a zombie apocalypse.

I realized that there were patterns there too. Patterns that revealed an underlying emotional need that made people keep things they didn't want but encouraged them to *buy things they didn't need.*

Our possessions fall into two categories: wants and needs. The needs are tools that make our lives simpler. A bed to sleep in, a frying pan to cook with, or a basic car to get us to work. And then, there are luxuries, which either elevate the tools or are things that we don't need but give us an emotional lift. Art on our walls, the tenth pair of black pants, or a fancier car to get us to work in style.

Where we get into trouble is when we find ourselves burdened by stuff, buying too much stuff, spending money we don't have on stuff, or thinking we have a right to stuff that is more than we truly need.

We are all vulnerable to these traps, for multiple reasons we will cover in depth. The goal of this book is to help you see if you are using your stuff to fill holes in your heart, head, or soul. Don't worry—I'm not going to tell you to give all your stuff away or stop shopping for the rest of the year, but I am going to help you become aware of why we shop. And with that awareness, how to change our behaviors and find fulfillment in healthier ways.

By getting to the root of this hidden scourge, we can redirect those emotional and financial resources toward real goals like True Connection, Free Time, and Self-Confidence.

In this book, I am going to introduce you to what I call the Seven Emotional Clutter Magnets. These are the empty parts of us that desperately want to attract one of seven important feelings: purpose, love, connection, wisdom, confidence, self-respect, and ease. These are the feelings that make us excited to get out of bed in the morning, and when they're missing in our lives, we actively try to pull them in, or "magnetize" them, if you will.

But sometimes these internal magnets get flipped and start pulling in stuff instead. As though the stuff could be a replacement for those feelings. That may work for a few minutes or hours. Like on days when you get to work too early knowing you also have to stay late, you convince yourself that a candy bar is just the break you need instead of an actual day off. Or how we grab a glass of wine to feel momentarily more relaxed, but that one glass (or three) isn't the solution to chronic stress. In both these examples, we are magnetizing a thing (the candy bar or wine) to fill an emotional need instead of being honest with ourselves about the deeper issue.

We will see chapter by chapter how overbuying *never* solves a Clutter Magnet. The pull of an activated magnet is not a well that can be filled but an emotional void that needs positive emotion to counter it. I often imagine these giant cartoon magnets in my clients' homes just sending out magnetic waves, drawing handbags and power tools and kitchen gizmos to them from across the universe. Forever. Until we turn the magnet off.

We are going to turn your Clutter Magnets off by first identifying the emotional holes that we are trying to fill and then, chapter by chapter, redirect that powerful pull toward stuff onto deeply and sustainably rewarding parts of life. You'll learn how to stop magnetizing "date night outfit" clutter and instead cultivate the love you really want to feel. Or stop magnetizing status symbols and learn to feel self-respect. All of which will cumulatively lead to a much happier emotional landscape. When we cultivate habits that nurture us and bring lasting joy, we can break these unhelpful patterns once and for all.

———————————

During the pandemic, we all peered into each other's homes like never before. Whether it was the boss Zooming in from her bedroom or the nation TikToking from their kitchen, we saw how other people are living—and it often wasn't pretty. But I have been here for the last fifteen years, intimately facing people's inability to maintain a functional relationship with their stuff.

Clutter is not a superficial problem. It's an emotional issue that requires an astute solution to help people attain life goals. Whether you want a greater sense of purpose, more social connection, or buckets of love, we are going to look at how you want to *feel* as you move through your day and why overbuying hasn't made you feel that way. Then, we'll figure out how to eliminate the clutter. Ultimately, these eight chapters aren't actually about personal organization— they're a road map to your personal fulfillment.

I'm so excited to go on this journey with you!

your 7 emotional clutter magnets

"Wanna fly, you got to give up the shit that weighs you down."

TONI MORRISON

FOOTBALL FIELDS OF NEW AND USED CLOTHES. Cargo containers of baby gear. Gymnasiums full of old towels and bed linens. Broken toys. Working toys. Bicycles, tricycles, and scooters. Books, books, and more books. I am a professional declutterer, and the amount of stuff I have helped people jettison over fifteen years could furnish all the homes in Vermont. Maybe twice.

And people do need help tackling clutter in their homes. Clutter is tenacious. It builds up slowly, we get used to living with it, and it can feel overwhelming to address. Not only that, but even things we're desperate to let go of just...linger. And this can have real consequences on our well-being. A 2017 study published in *Current Psychology* demonstrates that clutter and procrastination go hand-in-hand. People procrastinate decluttering, and then the overwhelming presence of the clutter leads to the postponing of other beneficial activities.[1]

My superpower is helping you see why you can't let go of the possessions that get in your way, slow you down, and stand between you and the life you want to be living.

In this book, I take this idea one step further. I start by examining who brought those possessions into your home: you.

No judgments. But so often my clients look around helplessly like a masked bandit has been bringing things in while they sleep. No. You (or someone you live with) bought or ordered or accepted everything in your home. Take a moment to sit with this. You brought everything into your home.

#Truth.

What's so awesome about this fact (once you've caught your breath) is that *you* are in the driver's seat. *You* are in charge of what comes into your life and your home. In this book, we are going to slow down on that part of the clutter cycle—the acquisition part—and dismantle it for good. No more ferrying bags to Goodwill only to watch your house fill right back up again.

To break that cycle, though, we need to first understand why we buy things. We may think we need them. But for many of us, the word "need" is a catch-all term for some unhelpful behavior patterns. Reexamining why we buy things is critical because healing Clutter Magnets isn't simple. It's a commitment that requires some deep dives into our habits, our coping mechanisms, the things we attract, and the things we avoid.

In order to succeed, we need to first look at what we're up against. Spoiler alert: it's a lot.

The History of Clutter

For the majority of human history, two things were precious and hard to come by: food and possessions. For thousands of years, we evolved to hoard what we came by when we came by it in anticipation of bad harvests and bad weather. We valued food we could dry or preserve, animal skins to keep us warm or provide shelter, and implements to manipulate the natural world into sustenance. All of it was precious because it was so labor-intensive to produce. Until the invention of candles, there were truly only so many hours in a day.

Then, a mere two hundred years ago, machines were invented—and *everything* changed. We take living in a mechanized and technological world for granted, and we forget that this is a recent phenomenon in human history. I was recently re-reading Laura Ingalls Wilder's *Little House on the Prairie* to my niece, and I was startled to be reminded of a world in which almost everything was made by your own two hands. Every stick of furniture, every tool and implement. The fabric and needles were bought, but the clothes were hand-sewn, handwashed, and laid out to dry. Due to the time and effort that went into making each item, no one had more than what they truly needed.

I bring this up because what happened over the past two hundred years is that we got very far away from the concept of "need." Generally speaking, we misuse the word entirely. "I need new leggings." "I need another skillet." "I need that $500 hair dryer."

Line up the last ten things you bought.
How many of them did you actually need?

Even through the 1900s, goods were expensive. If you were alive in the 1970s, you probably remember regularly polishing your shoes or getting your shoes resoled so they would last longer. You might remember how important your birthday wish list was because you wouldn't be given anything else until the holidays. You might remember darning socks, wearing hand-me-downs, or buying goods on layaway. We learned skills to care for our stuff because it was valuable.

My grandmothers taught me to sew so I could replace a button, make a simple quilt, or even whip up my own prom dress in all its lavender satin, puffy-sleeved '80s splendor. Every summer, I used to go to Arizona to visit Grandma Frieda for a few weeks before I went back to school, and we would sew a new quilt for my bed. We would sit on the floor, quilting and talking. My other grandmother, MM, taught me to reaffix loose buttons, mend small holes, and use tape to make a hem. The time I spent sewing (and cooking and gardening) with my grandmothers was so special. In addition to learning a valuable skill that has served me well, it was also a chance to connect with them and hear their childhood stories. As we stitched, I learned what it was like for them to live through the Depression, two world wars, and the advent of everything from the Model T car to the computer.

Learning how to sew also taught me how many resources go into one article of clothing, from material to time. It's like the first time you bake anything from scratch. I used to eat scones with wild abandon because they are stinking delicious. And then I decided to make a batch from scratch. That's when I learned how much butter goes into each scone. Hence the deliciousness. And I realized that scones are not the healthiest things to eat daily. So now, when I occasionally eat a scone, I am making an informed food choice and enjoy it very, very much. It's the same with sewing clothes. When I became aware of how difficult sewing a button-down shirt from a bolt of fabric and a pattern was, it gave me a great appreciation for every piece of clothing I buy. Someone had to mill the fabric and send it to another factory, and more people had to cut and sew the fabric into a shirt. Then that shirt had to be shipped to a store for me to buy. Clothing doesn't magically appear at the mall.

In the 1980s, there was yet another seismic shift in consumer culture: manufacturing moved to Asia, and the cost of goods plummeted. Rapidly, in a world where many Americans anticipated a shift from a forty-hour workweek to fifty and then sixty, investing time to repair things stopped making sense because you could just get a new one for a few dollars. Our time became incredibly constrained, and everything—clothes, home goods, shoes, office supplies—became not just inexpensive, but cheap.

Ridiculously cheap.

The dwindling price of goods removed an enormous barrier to consumption. And we are living with the consequences of this today.

Environmentally, global shipping for every T-shirt, can opener, and dishwasher added an enormous carbon footprint to everything in our homes. Plus, as the cost went down, the quality went with it and the cycle from purchase-to-landfill became stunningly short. Launched in 2019, the UN now has an Alliance of Sustainable Fashion because the industry is the second-largest consumer of water and is responsible for 10 percent of global carbon emissions, more than all international flights and maritime shipping combined. Meanwhile, the average consumer buys sixty more pieces of clothing annually than they did fifteen years ago—and they keep them for half as long.[2]

The United States alone creates 292.4 million tons of municipal solid waste a year, and landfills are quickly becoming one of the biggest contributors to climate change. Much of this is caused by our overconsumption of cheap consumer goods.

From an equity standpoint, very few factory workers in the developing world where these goods are manufactured are paid a living wage, even relative to their cost of living. And lastly, vast swaths of America have turned into manufacturing wastelands. Every country used to have a sense of pride in making items specific to that country. Shoes from Italy. Pots and pans from France. Cars from the United States. But now that all manufacturing is outsourced to a few countries, we've lost a personal and prideful connection to our things. If you knew the person who made your napkins, you would hang onto them longer. You would not, instead, fill your sideboard with anonymous, mass-produced tableware that you can buy and dispose of without a second thought.

Everything has a price. Yes, you paid for the $3.99 T-shirt. But I am also paying for your $3.99 T-shirt. As is the woman who made it, the man who shipped it here, and the ocean it glided over. We are all paying in many ways, but if your home feels crowded, inefficient, or unsupportive because it is so crammed full of stuff, then you are paying for that T-shirt again and again.

Our homes are so full that we even shell out money for off-site storage units to house the things we think we need. A ten-billion-dollar-a-year industry around junk removal has sprung up in the last few years. Let that sink in: ten billion dollars a year is spent on hauling old stuff away.

Of course, there is also a well-being cost to all this excess, which is what we'll be focusing on in this book. At a minimum, clutter has been shown to raise our baseline cortisol levels, meaning all this profusion doesn't make us feel safe and secure—it stresses us out. Many people couldn't take psychological refuge in their homes during lockdown because their clutter was increasing their stress levels. Studies have also shown that clutter undermines the foundational sense of well-being we should get from our home. That sigh of contentment that we should be able to let out at the end of the day when we go through the door.[3]

This is not the path to happiness. For us, our families, our communities, or our planet.

How They Sell

In addition to consumer products being inexpensive relative to the median American income, why else do we buy more than we need? We are being prompted to do so all day, every day, through sophisticated advertisements.

Before we talk about the ads, we need to talk about something we are missing that would protect us. This thing is so basic and yet most people have no idea it even exists or that they are operating without it: media literacy.

I heard you say, "What?!"

Most of us went to American public schools that did not teach us how to be critical consumers of advertising and news. The consequences on the news front could not be more obvious or more dire with the proliferation of misinformation pitting states and families against each other. And the consequences on the advertising front are no less scary; it's leaving my clients to have unprotected sex with their news feed.

Media literacy is the ability to ask, "Wait a minute, but does it *really*...(remove stains/wrinkles/pet dander)? Have they *really*...(solved tooth stains/belly fat/melasma)? Who am I getting this information from? How does this benefit them? How can I cross-check and verify their claims? Who is making money off of my attention right now?" Think back to your last online purchase. Did you ask *any* of these questions? Did the product do what you hoped it would?

See how defenseless we are?

Now compound that with the fact that, before social media, we were only marketed to on television, on the radio, and in print media. Our homes were fairly neutral, ad-free spaces. Now, with most of us glued to our phones all day, we are seeing *thousands* more ads each week than we did ten years ago.

Even worse, these ads are designed to disarm us.

They look like a friend filming a genuine product rave from their bathroom. Or maybe an influencer we trust sharing a new product they *love*. We stop and watch. Wow, her eyelashes look *amazing*. Her couch is *so* clean. That blouse is *crazy* flattering! And it's only $42! Click, click, click—done.

In the aughts, I had a friend who produced infomercials. We loved hearing her stories about faking results on set. "Well, we pre-chop the vegetables." "We swap the new tiles out for the old tiles." "That's not grease, it's actually lube with food coloring, so it comes right up."

Those same people are now producing these influencer ads. (And make no mistake, these ads are produced.) BECAUSE THEY STILL NEED YOU TO BUY THEIR PRODUCT.

That might seem obvious, but everything about these ads is designed to obscure that fact. What you *feel* is that someone is sharing an insider tip on a product that will make your life better. They are trying to *help* you.

No.

This person is paid to pretend *not* to be an actor, to look like someone who just needs to let everyone know how great their skin looks today for no reason. The company paying that actor NEEDS TO MOVE PRODUCT to stay in busi ness, and they will pretty much do that by all means necessary. That means populating their website with hugely doctored pictures of their clothes, binder-clipping the back of every dress to make it fall perfectly, and getting makeup artists to pretend to be ordinary people who can apply false eyelashes in seconds.

Here's the bottom line: there is no magical catch-all

product. If someone had discovered the antidote to aging, they wouldn't be advertising on Instagram and selling it for $39.99.

Also, these companies are hoping you're too busy to return anything that didn't work as advertised. I have countless clients with mud rooms or car trunks full of packages that were supposed to be returned. My local resale shop is full of clothes with the StitchFix labels still attached.

Almost all subscription boxes are basically 1-800-GOT-CLUTTER. In 2019, the dog toys and skinny jeans and skincare samples started rolling in, and most of my clients found themselves trapped in a Möbius strip if they tried to unsubscribe. "We're sorry, you agreed to a one-year term that has already auto-renewed." And some even have return policies that translate to: "Gotcha, sucker!"

Worse, even if you manage to return the product, it may just get thrown out. A 2020 investigation by Basel Action Network, an environmental justice nonprofit, found that Amazon resells only 30 percent of its returned merchandise. The rest is destroyed, thrown out, or warehoused to be re-sold to a third-party seller in bulk because that's cheaper than re-packaging and re-shipping it. But the environmental impact of this policy is huge. The carbon footprint of a simple printer doubles when it is shipped, returned, and then dumped in a landfill.

> If you take anything away from this book,
> please check return policies before every
> purchase. If returns aren't allowed, that is a
> flashing, neon buyer-beware sign. They suck
> us in with pretty pictures and "vulnerable"
> videos and then send us the equivalent of
> an exploding snake in a peanut brittle can.

Now let's look at why we're so vulnerable to all this.

Why We Buy

Buying things feels good!

I'm sure that will be the least surprising sentence in this whole book. We all know that. But why? *Why* does handing over money or swiping a card make us feel momentarily happy?

First, from a neuroscience perspective, shopping releases a tiny hit of dopamine, our pleasure and reward hormone. We run to the store and get lemons and olive oil, and our brains reward us with an itty-bitty boost of self-soothing.

Why are we wired this way? It goes back to the cycles of food abundance and starvation. When food is plentiful, we are cued to *keep acquiring*. Gather *all* the berries. Harvest *all* the grain. Hunt *all* the meat. And then store everything to get you through the winter.

Humans who didn't have that drive did not survive to pass on their genes. And then, as civilizations developed, hierarchies were formed based on who had *more*. More land, more wives, more cattle, more grain. Add to that how hard it was to acquire anything—"You want a cup? Great! Find the right mud, mold it, dry it, paint it, and hope it doesn't fall apart!"—and it was good that our brains got us a little high to reward us for persevering.

But when was the last time you made anything? Or grew anything, for that matter?

We can now have whatever we want whenever we want wherever we want it, but our brains have not caught up. They are still rewarding us for buying a back scratcher as if we just built our first table.

So, know that you are going to feel momentarily good after paying for that exercise ball, shampoo, or cocktail dress because that's what our brains wired us to do: keep acquiring the things that would keep us safe. But that does not mean that buying that item was good for you.

We have these external cues working on us, in the form of near-constant advertising pressure, and we have the internal cues, in terms of the dopamine hit when we buy.

But we also have the conscious decision-making part of our brains pushing us to buy as well.

When life feels scary, overwhelming, or just generally stressful (which I think most of us can agree has been approximately every day for the last however many years), it is tempting to distract ourselves with a project. We want to take control and we think we can solve all our problems by *buying* something.

Let's re-do the den. Let's get a better car. The kids killed the couch. I need a top that can go from Pilates to the office—or Zoom. There is a problem. I have to solve it.

The next thing we know, we are on a Pinterest ram page trying to solve a problem by planning an acquisition that will "fix it." Even declutterers are now selling clutter in the form of "organizing products." You know what makes a great drawer divider? An old shoe box. And here's the big secret all the professional organizers with their own product lines aren't telling you: no number of bins and baskets will get you organized if you have too much stuff! I recently saw that a very popular pair of organizers now have a clothing line. Comfy, around-the-house clothes to color code in. Like the shoe box, a good pair of jeans works to tackle any organizing project.

But again, instead of the hard work of clearing out the clutter and confronting the emotional blocks that could come up, it's easier to go to the mall and come back with, say, even more shopping bags full of acrylic.

And if that acrylic is on sale?! I mean, you would be a fool *not* to buy it! When goods were expensive, sales and coupons really helped families stretch a dollar to ensure everyone had shoes that fit and full bellies. The concept of saving money on necessities was a real thing.

Today, sales are constant and fairly meaningless. If everything is on sale, nothing is on sale. And yet we continue to boast about getting something on sale as if we caught wild game. Marketers use that to their advantage. Most department stores anticipate their seasonal sales and double their mark-ups. Then, when the sales roll around, they slash the prices down to the profit margin they originally needed. Or look at outlet malls. That is their entire business model. Most of the goods for sale there are not the marked down "extras" but second-rate goods manufactured for the outlet malls to be marked up, and then marked down.

Be mindful of how we are encouraged to buy more than we need. "Buy one, get one half off!" Do you need a second one? Can you use the first one before the second goes bad? Often the price for buying just the one will still be reduced. "Two packages for $5.99!" How much is one packet? $2.99. No actual savings for buying two.

After I wrote my first book, I was hosting weekly

Facebook Live sessions for a few hundred regular participants in discussion about Emotional Clutter Blocks and Clutter Magnets. It's a lively group committed to healing the emotions that keep them trapped with stuff they don't want. When I pointed out to them that those "holiday" bundle baskets are usually filled with the year's under-selling scents and that these promotions are just designed to clear products no one wanted, one woman said to us, "I'm having a proud moment. Bath and Body Works had a tote filled with products for $35 with a $30 purchase. I had a $15 gift card. I figured it would be the perfect time to use it and get the tote full of stuff. Then I realized that I don't even know if I like the scents in the tote. I thought of using them as gifts for Mother's Day, but as I said, I don't know what they smell like. I realized that the 'bargain' would not be a bargain at all. It would be clutter that I would hang on to for years. Instead, I've decided to put my gift card toward hand soaps with a scent I like because that's what I really love and will use."

A bargain is not a bargain if you never use it!

Another reason we don't use the stuff we have already bought is a phenomenon called "the specialness spiral." Research published in the *University of Chicago Press Journal for the Association of Consumer Research* explains how it works.[4] Essentially, if we buy something, say a candle, and the first time we have an impulse to light it and we *don't*, we imbue the item with additional value. It becomes special. We need to save it for a worthy occasion. Fast forward to the next bath or dinner party or work event, and now we decide that no event is worthy of the item. There could be a better occasion coming up and we don't want to waste this precious thing on just any bath or dinner party or work event. Fast forward another year—or two. The candle now has no smell. You paid for the item and stored it at home. And because of the specialness spiral, you essentially turned it into a bunch of bananas that over-ripened and had to be thrown out.

I recently bought a pair of jeans online and, after trying them on, promptly returned them. When the company received the jeans, they started sending me emails saying, "Hurry, you have a credit waiting. It's going to expire soon!" The credit was my money in the first place. With no expiration date. They reworded my return to look like it was a special offer. Sneaky, huh?!

I'm just trying to begin to shift your thinking because one of the most helpful practices for changing our consumer habits is simply starting to get some perspective on these cues that make us shop. Just layering in the awareness that we are being marketed to can change how we engage with social media. Maybe we can start automatically scrolling past the ads without even letting our eyes and brains engage. Or rolling our carts past buy one, get one half off signs. Do you need to buy something to solve your problem? Is that sale an actual savings? Or is it just luring you to buy something you don't need?

Look, my old apartment was an open loft, and I tried a lot of different configurations with a bookshelf I already owned before I figured out the exact layout to make the space feel divided. And that meant buying a different piece of furniture. I'm not saying that we never need new things. That we never have problems to solve.

I am saying that frequently I find clients wrestling with a problem that can't be solved by shopping—like caring for an aging parent or helping a teenager with learning challenges—and instead they focus on what feels manageable, like tricking out the kid's room to look like the Enterprise or buying the parent a lot of gadgets that never get used.

So, before we even get to the Clutter Magnets, I want you to start asking if there is a larger, thornier issue you might be avoiding when you swipe your card.

The Donation Myth

The other reason we tend to buy with such abandon is that we are addicted to the donation myth. When I point to a large mound of unused items in their homes, clients will often say to me, "Oh, that's for donation."

We justify our purchases by telling ourselves that if we don't like them, we can just donate them. I hate to break it to you, but you probably won't. That item will probably just become clutter.

Thrift shops are full. They don't want your grandparents' furniture or tchotchkes or china. And we also tell ourselves that we can just sell the thing. But eBay doesn't want our stuff either. You will spend more mailing the Beanie Babies or Precious Moments figurines than you will get for them.

And with clothing so cheap, the secondary market for basic clothing is also rapidly dwindling. If you can get a pair of new jeans for the same price, why would you buy second-hand? We are incentivized to buy new.

The same is true for recycling. As of the writing of this book, the global recycling program is broken. According to the Environmental Protection Agency (EPA), of the 267.8 million tons of municipal solid waste generated in 2017, only 94.2 million tons were recycled or composted. Since 2018, when China stopped buying our plastic, U.S. processing facilities and municipalities have had to pay to recycle or be forced to discard it. In 2017, Stamford, CT, made $95,000 by selling recyclables; in 2018, it had to pay $700,000 to have the same materials removed. Bakersfield,

CA, used to earn $65 a ton from its recyclables; after 2018, it had to pay $25 a ton to get rid of them. Franklin, NH, had been able to sell its recyclables for $6 a ton; now the transfer station charges $125 a ton to recycle the material or $68 a ton to incinerate it.[5] Look at the TerraCycle model. It's a great way to recycle, but you have to pay to use their service. So, we pay to buy, and then we pay to remove.

If you blithely buy with the idea that these items may only be in your house for a little while before moving along to their next life, know that their next life is most likely a landfill.

Why Buying Doesn't Make Us Happy

We know this. We *all* know this. We have seen enough celebrity behind-the-scenes and where-are-they-now shows to know that unhappy people who run out and buy and buy and buy are still unhappy people. Just with multiple castles to mope around in and thousands of pairs of shoes to wear while they stare at their equally unhappy exotic pets. Know that you are not alone—very famous, successful people have fallen into this trap. If you are reading a clutter book, we can agree that you or your family have acquired stuff to the point where your home, and possibly your life, is no longer manageable.

Whatever you bought didn't do the trick.

It didn't do the trick because what we want is the *feeling* we think that item will give us. We want to feel younger, more successful, more desirable, more on our game.

> We don't want the item.
> We want the **FEELING** we
> think the item will bring.

The problem is that, while we may feel safe or loved or desirable or organized in the store or while we're staring at our phone, rarely does that feeling follow us home. But the clutter does. What I have found is that if we can identify the underlying yearning dictating people's clutter patterns, we can address that emotional need and then do the real work of magnetizing what they *really* want to be feeling.

The Seven Emotional Clutter Magnets I have identified are:

Clutter Magnet #1: *True Connection*, which is our primal need for tribe and community;

Clutter Magnet #2: *Strong Self-Confidence*, which is our belief in our inherent attractiveness, both to others and ourselves;

Clutter Magnet #3: *Free Time*, which is the knowledge we can move through life with ease and calm;

Clutter Magnet #4: *Big Love*, which runs the gamut from romantic to familial, and where some of our deepest wounds lie;

Clutter Magnet #5: *Self-Respect*, the knowledge that we bring unique attributes into the room, even without any status symbols to telegraph them;

Clutter Magnet #6: *Real Purpose*, meaning our craving for professional or vocational fulfillment; and finally,

Clutter Magnet #7: *Lasting Wisdom*, the confidence in our ability to implement all we have learned.

When my client has a Clutter Magnet, they are running up against their inability to stop overbuying to cultivate a feeling. They are yearning for something intangible, like self-confidence, and that yearning gets shifted onto stuff— creams and serums and shapewear. Instead of attracting more love or a greater sense of purpose, they call me because they are bringing in all this…garbage. They pull it with a seemingly unstoppable force into their homes and lives.

Once the flavor of their clutter points to the corre- sponding magnet, I ask them, "How can you *feel* respected, irrespective of what purse you're carrying?" Or "Can you *feel* connected to your grandchildren without buying them a cartful of toys every time you visit?" Now that we understand what it is we want to feel, we can begin to choose the *actions* that reinforce those feelings instead of the possessions. Because behaviors—not things—reinforce positive feelings. If they did, we would all only own one of everything.

> Behaviors—not things—
> reinforce positive feelings.
> If they did, we would all only
> own one of everything.

On a recent Facebook Live session, Anne, one of my regular participants, asked the group to support her in letting go of her collection of crafting kits.

"Crafts?" I asked to clarify.

"No, my collection of kits. To make crafts. Unopened. I have dozens of them. Including this unmade sock monkey kit that's just sitting on the counter."

I asked her what emotions came up when she thought about getting rid of them. She said, "I just feel like a failure! My mother was crafty, all my sisters are crafty, my nieces are crafty, and I live alone and can't even make a sock monkey!"

Crafting was clearly entwined with her idea of what it meant to be a successful woman. Then I asked her, "Do you want to make a sock monkey?"

"Well," she said tentatively, "No."

"Anne," I said, "What else do you do to give yourself a sense of self-confidence?"

"Well...I—I mean, currently I'm working on the issue of border detention. I'm a lawyer, but our role now includes ensuring these children are treated humanely until we can get them out. I'm doing everything from filing briefs to fund-raising for diapers."

There was a moment of silence as we all processed this.

"OK!" I said. "I give you permission to stop buying crafting kits to make you feel accomplished. And the next time you are tempted to buy one, I want you to say, 'I do not need to do this craft to feel good about myself. The work I do is so important, and at the end of the work-day, I deserve downtime that replenishes and relaxes me. Making potholders and sock monkeys is not it. And that's A-OK.'"

She felt enormously relieved.

Since our session, she has donated the kits to a local after-school program, she has not been to a Michaels in over a year, and she has moved on with her amazing life. By releasing the need to compare herself to her family and instead learning to celebrate all the ways she is valuable, she was able to heal the hole that she had been filling with crafting kits.

Summing It Up

My clients, readers, and followers who overbuy or over acquire are looking externally for a sense of purpose, connection, confidence, and love. They *want* to stop overbuying, but they don't know how because they don't know why they do it. Understanding the Clutter Magnets is the answer. Because the feeling won't be in the next Amazon box.

In this book, we are going to do the same work. We will figure out what you *truly* want to attract into your life and turn that magnet onto actions that create real, sustainable change. When we minimize our consumption, we maximize our outcomes.

2

magnetize true connection

"We're all just walking each other home."

RAM DASS

MAGNETIZING TRUE CONNECTION IS A FUNDAMENTAL human need, but we are lonelier than ever. Even before COVID-19 created a global pandemic, Western civilizations were becoming increasingly individualistic and isolated over the past few centuries. A 2020 report published by the National Academies of Science, Engineering, and Medicine reveals that more than one-third of Americans over forty-five feel lonely, and nearly one-fourth over sixty-five are considered socially isolated, meaning that they don't have enough social contact or regular interaction with other people.[1] I see this often with my clients in their seventies and eighties, some of whom have me over more often simply because they enjoy the company. As much as I love hearing their stories, I now make addressing their social connectivity part of our work together, so that by the time I leave, they have a plan to get out of the house and meet some folks.

I do this because, aside from the emotional toll of isolation, researchers are increasingly proving that social isolation has a high health toll as well. Isolation significantly increases a person's risk of premature death from all causes and is associated with a 50 percent increased risk of dementia and higher rates of depression, anxiety, and suicide.

Biologically, humans are pack animals. Our survival once depended on moving as a unit, and for thousands of years, families and communities roamed together. Then we lived and farmed together, eventually building villages and towns together. Generations lived under one roof or only a farm or two away.

Then came the industrial revolution. In the 1800s, thousands left the countryside for brutal, but better paying jobs in cities, and families were dispersed to wherever paying work could be found. Europeans immigrated to America in waves, and Americans began to look to the new Western frontier. The tight knit communities rapidly eroded. Once air travel was invented, it became all too common for parents to raise their children, only to watch them settle across the globe.

Many of my clients are somewhat stunned to find that, after raising their big families, none of their children live nearby. And to find that the grandchildren they thought they'd help raise are thousands of miles away.

I also have clients who thought they were making a responsible decision in their sixties to sell their giant homes and move to warmer, dryer places for retirement. What they discounted, though, was *community*.

My client Ellen had raised her family a couple hours south of Chicago, Illinois. Her husband had been a professor at the local university, and they had enjoyed a thriving social life. What they hadn't enjoyed as they aged were the bone-chilling temperatures and blowing snow.

Shortly after they retired to Scottsdale, Arizona, Ellen's husband, Howard, was diagnosed with Parkinson's disease, which progressed rapidly. Ellen found it very hard to make friends with other couples because she perceived that her husband's palsy made other people uncomfortable. She found herself extremely isolated with someone who couldn't do the things they had moved there for—golf, tennis, hiking.

When I arrived at Ellen and Howard's house at their son's behest, I found a lovely single-story home that had become impassable. Ellen had started buying in bulk everything she anticipated she would eventually need to take care of Howard—disposable mattress pads, adult diapers, washcloths. She had bought two kinds of walkers, a wheelchair, a motorized scooter, and a motorized wheelchair—none of which were needed yet.

When I asked about the boxes preventing her husband from moving around safely, she said, "I'm trying to get ahead of it." Buying all the things he may need someday made her feel materially prepared for something she couldn't emotionally prepare for.

Then I asked her what *she* needed, and I expected her to say "Help." I thought she might have been subsuming her need for help into marathon Amazon sessions. Instead, she said, "I need to get out more often. I'm afraid he's going to die, and I won't have any companionship."

Back in Illinois, she and her girlfriends had regularly gone to the theater or out to dinner. She used to belong to a book club and a cookbook club that met monthly to cook dishes by a famous chef.

I asked her about finding new people to do those things with in Arizona, and she said, "Those friendships started when our kids were little. Those women were my neighbors, my colleagues, my PTA buddies. How am I going to meet new people at my age?"

This is a fundamental flaw in our thinking that we can make at any age. *Everyone at this kindergarten or camp or college or sorority or branch arrived before me, and they've all paired up for life—I've missed it.* First off, you did not miss anything. If everyone is new in the situation, I promise that they're all as nervous as you are. Second, remember how excited you were in the past when someone new arrived and shook things up? That is how excited they are that you joined their dance class or community meeting or volunteer organization. We are social animals, and we love meeting new people once we get over our own fear of rejection.

I pointed out to Ellen that she might need to shift her thinking to help her get over the hump. She was someone who exercised regularly, ate well, and kept up with her checkups. With her husband's health deteriorating, hers became even more important. In the Harvard Longitudinal Study, the longest-running study ever conducted to evaluate the impact of our life choices on happiness, scientists began tracking the health of 268 college sophomores in 1938.[2] After following the men for nearly eighty years, researchers discovered that the key predictor of health and happiness in old age was close relationships. Those emotional ties help delay mental and physical decline and are better predictors of long and happy lives than social class, IQ, or even genes.

> We are social animals, and we love meeting new people, once we get over our own fear of rejection.

Dr. Robert Waldinger, one of the leading scientists to study the data from the Harvard study, said in his popular TED talk that "The people who were most satisfied in their relationships at age fifty were the healthiest at age eighty. Loneliness kills. It's as powerful as smoking or alcoholism."

In Dr. David Snowdon's pioneering longitudinal study of 678 nuns aged seventy-five and older, postmortem dissections revealed that a lack of social connectivity was a stronger predictor of how dementia would manifest than actual changes in the brain. The more social activities the nuns engaged in, the more backup neural connectivity they could rely on, even if they had Alzheimer's disease and much of their circuitry had been ravaged. Essentially, regardless of the actual amount of plaque on their brains, if they remained socially engaged, playing bridge and doing activities with others, they tended to display very few symptoms.[3]

The lesson here is to not let your friendships slip away. If you've uprooted yourself later in life, make planning to create friendships as much a part of your move as finding a new pharmacy or primary care physician. If you find yourself in a new place, pay attention to how and where you spend your time. Are you running to the grocery store or Target daily, buying stuff you don't need? Are these shopping trips making you feel like you've connected with other folks or seen familiar faces? If the buying has become the activity, this is the second Clutter Magnet in full effect.

What Stands in the Way

My clients who are craving more True Connection in their lives but are magnetizing clutter are using shopping either to connect or to avoid connection. Let's look at both.

Overshopping to magnetize True Connection is a tricky Clutter Magnet because shopping can frequently provide superficial engagement that masquerades as something more fulfilling. I work with so many widows and divorcees who build their days around buying and returning stuff. From clothes to home decor to so-called life solutions, they create projects for themselves to give their lives structure. But what they really crave is the human interaction they find during the transactions. They have a woman at the makeup counter who calls them when there's a new product launch or a free facial. They have managers at every boutique within a twenty-mile radius calling to let them know the season's new looks have arrived. The specialty store calls to say that the Italian rosemary crackers are back in stock. At each stop, they have a captive audience giving them undivided attention.

This is not a coping mechanism exclusively for the affluent. This also goes down at Walgreens and T.J.Maxx. I have a friend who linked his mother's debit card to an app on his phone. He saw that she was going to the drugstore several times a day, repeat buying aspirin and chewing gum just to give her day some structure. She finally allowed him to sign her up for classes at her local community center, where she made friends and shifted the focus of her day from imagined needs to engaging with others. Now her mental life is busy remembering birthdays and knitting gifts for her friends.

The most insidious manifestation of this Clutter Magnet is the codependent variety. In her groundbreaking book *Codependent No More*, Melody Beattie identified a pattern of behavior where people put others' needs ahead of their own to an unhealthy extent. Typically, these are people who, as children, had to step into a caretaking role with their own parents beyond what is conventionally expected. Some of these responsibilities could be simple socioeconomic necessity, like caring for younger siblings while parents were at work, or sometimes there may be addiction or mental illness in the household. Regardless, they have been overfunctioning for others.

Codependent behaviors include feeling responsible for others, feeling compelled to solve the problems of others, overanticipating the needs of others. Saying "Yes" when you mean "No," doing things for others that they are capable of doing for themselves, feeling that you spend your whole life giving without reciprocity, and having an overwhelming desire for acceptance and affection.

What this looks like in relation to this Clutter Magnet is the codependent behavior of foisting unsolicited help on others. In the case of my clients, that means deciding that their adult children need a new wok, juicer, or slipper chair, and then sending it or dropping it off without asking. When the adult son or daughter is then irritated instead of thankful ("Mom, we don't drink juice!" "Mom, we are saving that corner for a desk that we need. Not a useless slipper chair!"), the parent feels rejected—an uncomfortable feeling they can only discharge by—you guessed it—more shopping.

Many of my clients have codependent baby boomer parents, and they feel endlessly flummoxed. "I don't understand. I didn't ask her for a new quilt, and now she's so angry at me!" That is their codependence pushing them to buy things that no one asked for. Their magnetic need for True Connection causes them to buy, buy, buy stuff that no one needs or wants.

One of my clients, Amy, grew up terribly poor in the Ozark Plateau, so she loved that after decades of building a successful business, she could freely shop for her kids and grandkids. The only problem was—and I knew this because her grown children were also my clients—she had not taken the time to find out who they really were, what their tastes were, or what they needed. Ninety-nine percent of her gifts went straight to the thrift store or the garbage. It was a colossal waste of time and money. And terrible for the planet to boot.

Even worse, these acts of generosity drove her daughters further away, rather than bringing them closer. The resentment built as she showed up over and over with stuff her daughters didn't want, didn't ask for, and wouldn't use. Quickly. Nothing feels good about being gifted a bunch of throw pillows that don't go with your decor just because someone else felt like shopping. Unwanted gifts aren't gifts—they are clutter. They are just one more thing to deal with, make a decision about, and ultimately get rid of. Every time Amy's car pulled into the driveway, her daughters' hearts fell. They weren't excited to see their mother; they dreaded what she would bring with her.

Last holiday season, I staged an intervention. First, I pushed Amy to sit down with a year's worth of credit card statements and tally what she spent every year on random stuff she saw ads for in her feed. She was stunned by the number. Because she was buying in increments of $4.99, $14.99, and even $24.99, she was still being frugal while being generous. Somehow honoring her heritage while also defying it. However, the reality was that those tiny numbers added up to thousands of dollars between her two daughters, their spouses, and five grandchildren. And no one had anything to show for it.

Patricia, her eldest daughter, was especially frustrated because her husband had lost his job and some strategic financial support would have been highly welcome. "Why can't she gift the girls their sports uniforms for next season instead of this oversized Hello Kitty lamp that burnt out after two weeks?!" she wailed to me.

At Amy's kitchen table I said, "This year, you are going to ask all the girls in every generation for a list, and you are going to get them the things they ask for—the things they will *use*. For two reasons. First, you will learn something about them when you take the time to look for the things they genuinely enjoy. That will bring you closer to them.

Two, by getting them something they really want and will use, they will think of you every time they put it on or put it out, and it will foster the closeness and connection you are looking for."

It was not easy. The plan went against all of Amy's instincts. But her daughter told me that it was the first Christmas she wasn't angry at her mother and the first January she didn't have to drive around trying to rehome unwanted gifts. Amy also learned that one of her grand-daughters was taking cooking classes, and they started cooking together over Zoom every week.

We all know someone like Amy—someone who has gotten their sense of self-worth from overextending to the point that they can no longer tell if their help is even wanted. They feel compelled to jump in and start helping, and that help often looks like sending things no one needs. Then they feel insulted when their action isn't appreciated.

On the flip side, I also work with people who shop to avoid connection. For example, and this is a cliché, but one I see week after week: home renovations can be the gateway to divorce. The initial impetus may have been having a joint project, a material investment in the future. *We're designing how we want our life together to look.* But I have seen couples spend months arguing over the design of the closet only to never end up sharing that closet. What really went on there?

Shopping for fixtures, tiles, fabric, and accessories is a giant distraction from the underlying issues in a marriage. First, the couple is able to avoid tough conversations they weren't having by focusing on where the TV should go. Second, renovations are legitimately stressful, so they are able to pretend that all the problems in their relationship were related to the house. But once they move in, they have to confront the truth.

I also see a lot of husbands who keep buying their wives jewelry to offset some extramarital action. It fools nobody. Or, similarly, I see parents who work incredibly long hours or travel for months at a time, who overbuy for their children to substitute for the time they are missing. Spoiler alert: it never makes up for it. Their magnetic compulsion to buy to assuage the guilt will never be enough.

A good use of your time and attention is spending time with the people you love. Peaceful, unprogrammed time. If the time with them isn't peaceful and rewarding, then the relationship needs work. And no joint project or purchase is going to fix that.

Similarly, I frequently see people who rely on shopping as their social activity primarily because it allows them to avoid real intimacy. We have a family friend in my parents' generation, let's call her Maggie, who has a hard time emotionally connecting with people, so she has always done it through shopping. Shopping becomes a safe parallel activity. You have a shared purpose, but it's also easy to move away from the other person without seeming rude. It's basically an adult version of what developmental psychologists call parallel play, where toddlers each happily do their own thing beside each other without interacting. Shopping allows Maggie to mill about in the vicinity of me or my nieces, lost in a totally separate realm of focus, and the merchandise gives her something to talk about without ever having to share how she's *really* doing. Or inquire into the well-being of whomever she's combing the racks with. She could achieve the same level of connection watching a movie alone.

If this concept feels familiar, I invite you to start separating the activity of seeing friends or family from the activity of shopping. Can you meet for a walk or a movie or a coffee? Can you play cards? Cook together?

Contact your friends and ask them what they have wanted to find more time for in their lives, and then see if you can support each other in doing those activities together. This strategy is what productivity experts call a "multiplier." It's not multitasking, where you split your attention, like trying to watch a movie and respond to emails at the same time. Before you know it, the movie isn't making sense and you clicked Reply All when you didn't intend to—ugh! A multiplier accomplishes two things at once because one activity doesn't require your active attention. For example, when you walk around the reservoir and connect with friends, you are using your time efficiently and getting two benefits from one activity. Walking also contributes to stress reduction and joyful longevity. When the *New England Journal of Medicine* followed 8,000 men over twelve years, they found that those who walked two miles a day had a nearly 50 percent reduction in mortality and had cut their risk of dying from cancer by 65 percent![4]

I was thinking the other night about what I would do if I got my grandmother back for just one day. Poof, she would appear, and I would know that we'd have a whole day together. I started thinking about what we would do, and do you know what didn't come to mind? Shopping! I didn't think about heading to the mall. I thought about sitting at her breakfast room table, drinking tea, and asking her a million questions about how she felt being a woman during the twentieth century. How it was raising a kid alone in the 1950s? All the things I could talk to her about to deepen our connection. I would want to know her better and understand our family better. I realized that all I wanted was True Connection.

Imagine someone who has passed that you miss deeply. Picture them coming back for a day. What would you spend that day doing? Taking a long walk? Eating your favorite meal? Talking late into the night? I am going to venture that you won't think, "I'm going to take this unbelievable opportunity and precious time and go to the Dollar Store to see what deals we can get."

Now, extend this imaginative exercise to someone alive. What could you be doing with them on a regular basis that would give you that feeling of connection? Having them over for a home-cooked meal? Preparing that meal together? Offering to go over to their house and tackling a project they need help with? Taking a class together? Most likely it's something you'd do face-to-face. Not shopping.

How to Nurture More Connection

If there is something we had driven home to us in 2020, it's that time with other people is precious. And essential. But, as in the case of Ellen, the Scottsdale transplant with the ill husband, admitting that you are craving more True Connection in your life can be scary because it requires vulnerability. It is so much easier to say, "I need new shoes," than "I need a friend."

But that is exactly where to start. Say it out loud even. See how good it feels to admit that. Because we can spend an enormous amount of energy trying not to feel uncomfortable feelings—like loneliness—which leads to leaning on unproductive coping strategies—like shopping—to avoid them.

If you suspect that you have been using shopping as a substitute for more meaningful interaction, there is a two-pronged solution. You have to reduce your habit of shopping to make space for more human engagement, but you also need to start reaching outside your comfort zone to either meet new people or engage with the people already in your life.

Let's discuss social media. Social media can make us *feel* like we're more connected. We see pictures of friends or their children or holidays, and we think we know something about their lives. But liking a post is no substitute for meeting a friend for a walk. I have a friend who always posted the greatest pictures of her kids skateboarding. There they'd be in Santa Monica at sunset, their blond hair blowing around their heads as they hovered, suspended in mid-air. It always seemed like she had the most enviable, fancy-free life. And then I ran into her at Trader Joe's and learned that her mother's dementia had rapidly worsened, that her sister was completely MIA, and that she was heartbroken to think of putting her mother in assisted living. I ended up taking her outside so we could sit on a bench and she could have a good cry. But it shouldn't have taken running into her in the frozen food aisle for us to have that moment. I should have reached out to her months earlier for a coffee or a walk, but I'd been under the impression that all was well.

The fact is that we all have something going on. We all need to talk, and we all need someone to listen. Social media *isn't* life. It's the highlight reel.

On his episode of Dax Shepard and Monica Padman's *Armchair Expert* podcast, Daniel Goleman, PhD, talks about the necessity of in-person socialization to boost our EQ, or emotional intelligence. He defines emotional intelligence as the ability to perceive, use, understand, and manage our emotions.[5]

A 2008 review published in the *Annual Review of Psychology* found that higher emotional intelligence is positively correlated with better social relations for both children and adults, higher social standing, better academic achievement, better social dynamics at work, and better negotiating ability. Finally, and most importantly for our purposes, this review found that emotional intelligence is positively correlated with higher levels of life satisfaction and self-esteem along with lower levels of insecurity and depression.[6]

But we don't develop emotional intelligence virtually! As Goleman says, "We are designed to learn from life,"[7] and not screens, meaning that our brains are wired to read people and learn from those interactions. That neural process doesn't happen when we look at photographs or chat online.

That's why it's so important to make sure that you have a robust community of real flesh-and-blood friends who want to meet up out in the actual world. It will take more effort than scrolling, but it will reward you emotionally, physically, and mentally.

Are you single, but all your friends have kids? Suggest meeting in the park so the kids can play, and you can talk. Offer a double activity. It can sound like this: "Let's meet for an hour and catch up, and then I'll take the kids home or out to lunch so you can get a manicure." Or plan a night out that a friend with young children can manage—start early and make a reservation so you don't waste precious time. Go to their neighborhood.

Are you new to town? Meet-ups are a great way to connect with new people. See if the local library hosts events or if the local bar has game nights. Or if your yoga studio hosts events. And get bold! Ask someone to get a drink or a coffee after class. If it's not a great match, then just smile and move on. You won't know until you stick your neck out a little bit.

A friend of mine moved for work from LA to Seattle, where she didn't know a soul. Before she went, she posted on Facebook: *Moving to Seattle next week. If you know any amazing, like-minded folks up there, would you set us up on a Friend Blind Date? Coffee, drinks, or a walk around the city?* The request was crazy successful, and within her first month, she had the beginnings of a great friend circle out-side of work.

Believe me, I know it all sounds exhausting. Just set the goal of trying one new activity or one new interaction each week. Buy an old-fashioned calendar and put it up where you'll see it. Give yourself a check mark on all the days when you talk to someone in real life either in person or on the phone, or when you try a new social activity or initiate a get-together. Challenge yourself to get an unbroken streak of connections. And if you have a few quiet days, don't beat yourself up but don't let yourself off the hook. Pick up the phone tomorrow and keep building those muscles. Strengthen the bonds of friendship instead of your shop-ping muscles.

Integrating Decluttering and Connection

If you have been overbuying instead of connecting, your clutter can become your ticket *out* of isolation. For my cli-ents who have been diverting their need for community into collecting, dispersing that collection can be a great way to initiate connection.

My client, Artie, had been collecting baseball cards for years, with the intention of passing the collection down to his grandkids. However, because the piles of boxes reached the ceiling of the spare room, the grandkids never spent the night. And because he was so protective of the cards, he didn't let his grandkids handle each one or teach them about why they were so special. A huge True Connection opportunity was missed.

I helped him get all the cards out of boxes and into albums, so that the kids could safely handle them. I helped him disperse the duplicates and the ones in poor condition, freeing up the spare room, and then I set him the goal of hosting the kids more and using the cards to connect and learn about their interests.

The last time I saw Artie, he had begun giving the albums of the cards to his grandkids, so they could each start their own collections. He takes them to trading card conventions and is building memories with them that will outlast the hobby. After poring over the cards, they realized that it would be fun to go see baseball games in person. They are planning a summer road trip to visit the home stadiums of their favorite teams, giving them more time together and more opportunities to connect.

If you have assembled a collection of things you care about, invite your children or grandchildren over and take them through it. Explain the history or story behind each item, where you got it, and why it's special to you. Then the items stop being tchotchkes and become a part of who you are and what you value. Dispersing a collection is a great way to reconnect with friends and family.

Bear in mind that your family may not want any of your collection, and that's OK. You collected because it was an enjoyable pastime to you, but you cannot foist this onto others no matter how hard you try. And understand that if roosters, miniature cars, or wind-up toys are not their thing, it doesn't mean that they don't love you. Post what you are letting go of on your local Buy Nothing group and pass it on to someone who will love those things as much as you do. In addition, Buy Nothing groups are another great way to meet like-minded people.

When I first moved to LA, I was dipping my toe in the acting world, which meant taking lots of acting classes and waiting tables at night. (I take a moment to bow to all the food and beverage servers out there! It can be such a thankless job.) While it was really tough living on tips, it was a great chapter in my life that I will always cherish. One of the best parts was a group of actresses in their thirties who befriended me and included me in their seasonal clothing swap, during which one person's discarded items became another's treasure. We weren't embarrassed to be wearing used clothes. In fact, we were proud of reusing clothing and saving money.

Four times a year, about ten women would drop off their

unwanted clothes to the host of the swap. We would go through our piles and hold them up article by article, talking through the pros and cons of each piece. Anyone interested in it would then try it on. If only one person wanted the item, they got it. If more than one person wanted it, the group would vote on who it looked better on, and that would determine the new owner.

One rule of the clothing swap was that no one was allowed to say disparaging things about their own or anyone else's bodies, so the voting process was incredibly kind and encouraging. In fact, we were always encouraging people to try things on that they otherwise might not have had the courage to. It was a love fest of positive female energy, and I made friendships that I still have to this day.

We became so much closer talking through our body issues and listening to the stories that went with the clothes—the bad dates, the good dates, and everything in between. That kind of bond couldn't have been created in a dressing room at Bloomingdale's.

I carried on the tradition for years, and to this day, friends still say, "Should we bring back the clothing swap?" We need to get back to this. Clothes don't need a price tag dangling from them to make us feel special.

If you have household clutter you need to unload, donating is a great way to start a relationship with an organization that could lead to volunteering and, thus, more human connection. Animal welfare organizations always need used, clean sheets and towels to make animal cages cozy. And they need people to walk the dogs or keep the cats socialized and ready for their forever homes. The foster care system is always in need of luggage to help kids safely move their belongings between homes too, and one simple donation could lead to a big brother or big sister role in a young person's life. These are just two examples of ways to turn your clutter into someone else's answered prayer and break the hold this Clutter Magnet has on you.

Summing It Up

How can you find True Connection without shopping? It may take a little bravery and putting yourself out there but as my grandmother always said, "You are never going to meet someone staying home." If you've just moved, jump on Nextdoor.com and see if there are any groups that interest you. Or set up a folding chair in your front yard in the evening and say hello to everyone taking their dogs out for a stroll. Magnetize new friendships, not more stuff.

Remember, your stuff can't love you back or ask you how your day was. And store employees are supposed to be friendly, but they are not your friends. They are there to sell you stuff. Sometimes we need the stuff, but often we do not. So don't accept items as stand-ins for relationships.

We all feel lonely sometimes, but instead of scrolling through Amazon for things you think you need, reach out to a friend. Chances are they need the human connection as much as you do. Find the people whose lives you will brighten, hold fast, and quickly you will break the second Clutter Magnet.

Once Ellen, my client's mother, donated the excess medical supplies to the local Arizona Red Cross, she was able to rearrange the apartment to better accommodate her husband's wheelchair. Once he could get around better, he was able to do more things for himself, and she was free to start volunteering one day a week and go out with her new friends one night a week. With the time she had previously spent shopping, she was able to research a local Parkinson's support group for both her husband and herself. He was engaged in ways she couldn't provide, and she was able to connect with other caregivers. "Tracy," she said to me, "It's a new lease on life. And it makes this new town feel like home."

3

magnetize strong self-confidence

"True belonging only happens when we present our authentic, imperfect selves to the world; our sense of belonging can never be greater than our level of self-acceptance."

BRENÉ BROWN

EVERLANE. VIOLET GREY. RITUAL. WHAT ARE THESE companies selling? Not clothes, skincare, or vitamins. What they are selling is confidence. *If you buy our [insert product], you'll feel better about yourself. You'll hide—or lose—that flaw that keeps you from feeling attractive. And having the life you aspire to. Is your hair lackluster? Do you have a muffin top? Wrinkles? Just click here, and your problem will be solved for good.*

Except when in the history of products being marketed to women (and it has traditionally been to women) has anyone bought anything and then thought, "Wow, all my problems are solved! I will never need to buy another thing for the rest of my life—all my life goals did, in fact, hinge on my split ends!" No. We tend to move right onto the next problem the next ad tells us we have and obsess about fixing *that*.

Now imagine that ad was a guy sitting on the sidewalk shouting, "Hey, lady! You have under-eye bags! Give me $12, and I'll fix it."

You'd think, "Ew, no. Go away."

But if it's a pretty young woman in your social media feed saying the exact same thing, you think, "Ooh, yes."

There is something inside all of us that craves a quick fix, and the health and beauty industries play right into it, leading to the third Clutter Magnet: magnetizing strong Self-Confidence.

Americans spend more on beauty and personal care than any other country in the world, reaching $92.8 billion in 2019 alone—nearly double the figure from fifteen years ago.[1]

Do you have a medicine cabinet bursting with creams and serums? Oceans of potions and lotions on the countertop and more under the sink? A makeup drawer—or seven?

Do you collect hair-styling tools that all kind of do the same thing? Do you buy tons of clothes that you think hide or accentuate one part of your body? Do you have a kitchen full of diet aids? Do you have more than one subscription supplement service?

Then welcome to the confidence chapter of this book, where we unpack where we get it, what erodes it, why we try to buy it—and where we can get it instead.

What Stands in the Way

In their *New York Times* bestseller *The Confidence Code: The Science and Art of Self-Assurance—What Women Should Know*, authors Katty Kay and Claire Shipman write that there is "a vast confidence gap that separates the sexes. Compared with men, women don't consider themselves as ready for promotions, they predict they'll do worse on tests, and they generally underestimate their abilities."

Some of the reason for this is upbringing. Women are socialized to fit in by putting themselves down. The Australians even have a term for failing to measure up or really, measure down, called "tall poppy syndrome." You know what happens to the tallest poppy? It gets mowed over. The takeaway is that you don't want to be the one who stands out.

Yet there's also a lot of research on subtle differences in male and female neurobiology. For example, studies have found that women's fear center, the amygdala, is more easily activated, leading us to be more likely to ruminate over what's gone wrong in the past.[2] And we have a larger anterior cingulate cortex, which is the part of the brain that helps us worry. Translation: if we felt self-conscious in the past, we will turn the upcoming event—the dance, the date, the interview—over and over in our minds until we find a "solution." Or an Instagram ad posing as the solution.

Then there are the hormones.

As Jennifer Finney Boylan, a professor at Barnard College, wrote of her transition from male to female in her forties, "I found that the first thing I lost when I started taking estrogen was a sense of invulnerability and confidence I had always had as a man. And what do I think when I look in the mirror—especially considering that I never used to think that much about my appearance at all? I think, *This needs to be dry-cleaned.* Or *This would look better if I lost five pounds.* Or *I can't wear this because the blouse that matches it is wrinkled.* Or *This would look better if I lost ten pounds.* Or *What was I thinking when I bought this?* Or *This would look better if I lost fifteen pounds.*"[3] The self-doubt and self-criticism seems to be baked into our molecular biology.

Think about how you feel immediately after an expedition to find the look that you think hides all your flaws and accentuates all your assets. After a makeover at the beauty counter, maybe a new haircut, and the new outfit in the trunk of your car, you feel like a million bucks. Then on the drive home, your cell phone starts ringing, and the same issues you had before the appointment creep back into your life. By the time you walk through your front door, you've forgotten about how good all the quick fixes made you feel.

It's so important to be aware of subliminal messaging rather than just playing along in a system that wants to keep selling us clutter.

Weight and Wellness

No industry profits off our insecurities more insidiously than weight loss and wellness. Billions of dollars are made every year in the U.S. thanks to marketing for diet plans and products. Pills and powders, including old-fashioned metabolism boosters and so-called nutritional supplements that promise the perfect blend of digestive enzymes to melt pounds away. Gadgets like plastic pants to help you sweat off weight and shaking dumbbells for what they coin as "passive" exercise. And then there's exercise equipment—

from FitBits, water bottles, weighted vests, and specialized sneakers for specific activities to TheraBands and foam rollers. I have decluttered it all.

I want to tell you a not-so-hidden secret: the financial model for these companies is something called "recidivism." Originally describing how quickly a previously incarcerated person would reoffend, it now applies to all manner of broken promises in the world of recovery. Meaning relapse. We'd like to think that a diet program's business model wants us to lose and keep off all our excess weight. Then when we look amazing, all our friends will ask us what we used and try it too. But no. They are not counting on that. Because less than 1 percent of people currently paying to lose weight in the United States lose that excess weight and keep it off. It would be a bad business strategy.

Instead, they are, in fact, counting on the regain so they can welcome you back, so they can *re*-enroll you and send you new boxes of shakes, powders, and shelf-stabilized meals. Sometimes annually.

As a woman living in Los Angeles—frankly, on planet earth—I fully understand the grip this marketing can have on us. The headlines scream from every magazine in the supermarket checkout line. Your pre-wedding workout! Your bikini body! Get your pre-baby body back! It's relentless.

For years, I was obsessed with getting to a made-up goal weight that I honestly cannot even remember deciding. But I had a number. And my proximity to or distance from that number ruled my mental state. I took endless spin classes. I followed every new cleanse fad that my friends told me about. I monitored my calorie intake, my carb intake, and my fiber intake. I went keto. I went vegan. I tried Atkins. I tried South Beach. And then one day (probably just because I'd been working really hard), I woke up at my goal weight and stayed there for a few months. Here is my report back from goal weight land: it did not change one thing about my life. Not. One. Thing.

> **Here is my report back from goal weight land: it did not change one thing about my life. Not. One. Thing.**

Women waste *so much* valuable time and energy worrying about appearances when we could be working to change our lives or the lives of others. As brilliant author Caitlin Moran says in her book *More Than a Woman*, "I don't think you can truly love other women if you do not love your own body. It is urgent, urgent work for both yourself and womankind—to learn to love your own adorable legs and fully functioning arms. And you must *never, never, never* allow yourself to start seeing your body as a collection of separate, problematic items—cankles, muffin top, bingo wings, cameltoe—for that is the tactic of a far-right polemicist: dividing a glorious whole into a series of sad, isolated ghettos and then pitching them against each other. It's all you, and it must, urgently, become your lifelong friend." I could not agree more.

One of the greatest joys of my business is senior downsizing because I get to spend time with people who served in Korea or Vietnam, or people who lived during Jim Crow and devoted their lives to the civil rights movement. But always the most interesting to me are the stories from women who were at the forefront of the women's rights movement. One client, Georgina, was one of the first women in Los Angeles to run an ad agency. She was so outstanding in her field and was the first woman to win the Ad Man of the Year in the early 1980s. Not only did they have to change the name of the award, but the ceremony itself had always been held at a men-only club in Downtown LA, and she wasn't allowed in the elevator! She had to take the freight elevator *in her ball gown* with a rolling cart of appetizers and tubs of ice. As she told it, she held her head high and made her entrance as if it was on the red carpet at the Oscars.

You would think that, with all that she accomplished, she would have been oozing with Self-Confidence. For the most part she was…except when we decluttered her closets and kitchen. Every As Seen On TV exercise and diet gimmick had found its way into her home. A Twist 'N Tone—a giant massager that was just a huge rubber belt that shook your insides loose—a ThighMaster, and stacks of books that had the words "crash diet" in the title. The products and gimmicks were endless. As we were decluttering, the doorbell rang, and an Amazon delivery person delivered the latest and greatest diet tea.

I said to her, "Georgie, after all these years, aren't you exhausted from trying to be the perfect weight? When do you get to rest on your laurels?" We called it a day, and when I came back the next morning, she said, "I couldn't stop thinking about what you said. I so rarely think about what I've accomplished with my business and who I was in the world, but I constantly think about my weight and having a perfect figure. I think that if I could just look like Bo Derek, then everything I have done will mean more." We both sat with the moment. Even at her age, she was still trying to magnetize confidence from a gadget.

The other area where I see clients constantly spending *so much* money and creating *so much* clutter is on products related to wellness. Wellness marketing is so sly and slick because…we all want to be well! We all want to feel better! We want to sleep better, digest better, perform better, and relax better. And sometimes, when we don't have the time or discipline to take the actions that would truly make us feel better, we buy a doodad instead. In reality, the things you can do to affect your wellness the most are not things you can buy. Going to sleep half an hour earlier is free. Adding more leafy greens to your diet doesn't make clutter. Seeing friends is one of the greatest ways to boost your health and well-being—take a long walk together and you will have just achieved wellness gold without spending a cent.

I have clients whose kitchens are bursting with half-used jars and canisters of supplements, bedside tables that double as a mini expired CBD dispensary, bathrooms with broken jade rollers and moldy dry brushes, and a meditation corner with rancid chakra oils and mismatched sets of angel cards. But a sense of wellness cannot be ordered from a website, and it does not have a money-back guarantee (read the fine print). It does not expire.

We live in a culture where wellness has become another avenue for rampant consumerism. Frequently, I will arrive at a client's home to help eighty-six an old regimen because a new one is on the way. Why? Health fads! Take Bulletproof coffee and celery juice as two recent examples. Remember when everyone, including Jimmy Fallon, was extolling the virtues of putting butter in coffee? And then entire brands grew up around selling prefattened coffee when you could just...make a cup of coffee and put a pat of butter in it.

What's worse, many of those companies quickly tried to leverage that into selling supplements because it's easier and cheaper to sell an existing customer more products than to recruit a new customer.

After that, my friends pressured me to start drinking celery juice for weeks. "Tracy, the pounds just melt off! I've never felt so alive. You have to buy my special celery juicer!"

I was curious. But there was no way I was buying a product just for juicing celery. That seemed absurd. Instead I bought...some celery. And put it in my trusty old blender. Strained it and drank it. Total cost was one bag of celery.

I'll tell you the result of my experiment: it tasted so gross that it made my whole morning sad, and after two days, I was in full gastric distress.

Thank God I had not invested in a gadget that only juiced celery!

Look, I am all for trying things. Life is about new experiences. But find a way to do it that costs as little as possible and doesn't involve committing to a new gadget or system. You don't have to spend a lot of money and make it a dare to stick with something. Inevitably, that layers shame on top of shame when you don't keep taking the Booty Blast class but paid for six months in advance, or you stop drinking the shakes that taste like chalk even though you have two more cases in the garage, or you realize you hate the voice on the InnerPeace app you bought a one-year subscription to.

> **You don't have to spend a lot of money and make it a dare to stick with something.**

Instead I'd like you to be able to move on and say, "Phew, thank God I only did a trial class!" or "So glad I asked for a free sample!" or "Glad I figured out how to make that myself." And back to the celery juice: it may work for some folks, but before you spend a fortune on a juicer that you don't have room for, try premade juice first. And if after a couple months of drinking the juice you feel a difference, consider buying a used gadget. You will find a gazillion used juicers for sale on Facebook Marketplace.

I promise you—we don't need to spend money to show we're committed to self-care.

How to Feel Great about You

So how do we magnetize strong Self-Confidence if we're not putting it in our shopping carts?

In 2021, I decluttered and organized for Marley, a long-time client I had first worked with when she was pregnant with her first child. Fast forward and her youngest of three was already off to kindergarten. I'd loved watching the family grow and helping them organize to fit their changing needs.

One of the best parts of my job is getting to know people and hear their stories because when you're going through someone's old pajamas and socks, you learn a lot. Marley was no exception; she was interesting, smart, and well-read and we'd always shared recommendations for books we loved and beauty products that *really* worked.

Her clutter issues had always stemmed from living in a small house and keeping a tight schedule. But I was shocked at the volume of new products in her bathroom. The countertop was buried under all the products. As she saw the look on my face, she squeaked, "Just wait till you open the drawers." I did, and my jaw dropped a little more. Please understand that I have seen it *all*, so when *I'm* shocked by stuff, it means something. It wasn't even that it was so much; it was that it was so much more than I had ever seen her have. It seemed like when everyone else was buying hand sanitizer, toilet paper, and dried beans in bulk, she'd been loading up on eye cream, Retin-A, and hyaluronic acid.

We sat on the floor, and I made her smell and feel each product. I said, "I've known you for a long time, and I have never seen you shop at this level. What is this really about?"

Marley was a trained hip-hop dancer, but when she started having kids, she moved away from performing and into teaching. She told me about how she had taken a huge gamble and opened her own studio. It was slowly taking off and then bam...the pandemic hit. By the time the studio could safely reopen, she had lost all momentum. She felt like a failure. Even though the pandemic wasn't her fault, she told herself that she was a terrible businesswoman, incompetent marketer, and now too old to be a performer. This is where all the potions and lotions came in. The business closing completely rocked her confidence, and she was trying to regain her youth with sheet masks.

As we talked it through, I helped her see that she was trying to buy confidence one lotion at a time. I helped her focus on all that she did in her amazing life as a mother of three kids, and we came up with ways she could use her dance training. So now, on the occasional Saturday, I head to our local park and take her outdoor cardio dance class. She has a big group of devoted attendees and fans, and as I was leaving the other day, I heard one of the students talking to her about a new space to rent. It sounded like the school would get back on its dancing feet!

Like Marley, in order to make the shift, we have to do the work in our heads. I think you know what I'm going to tell you because it's what the adults around you probably used to tell you during those self-loathing teenage years. You didn't believe them then, and you may not believe me now. But this is where self-doubt cluttering ends and Self-Confidence begins.

Self-Confidence is a muscle that we all have the capability to build, and it starts by believing that we all bring an individual spark to the world—a flavor that is uniquely us.

Take a minute and think about all the ways you are special. Are you an amazing cook and often share your culinary skills with others? Can you make people laugh? Are you quick with compliments and make strangers smile? This little bit of spice is what makes you special.

The world needs your spice, now more than ever, so spend some time thinking about how you are uniquely you. And remember:

You.

Are.

Awesome.

Without waterproof vegan eyeliner. Without a cleanse. With your current hair color.

Just awesome.

Loveable and desirable.

However, to make a significant change in your outlook—or in this case, I call it the "inlook"—you need to start believing that you are awesome, loveable, and desirable. It's incredibly simple, yet incredibly hard. That's why I want you to start devoting the time you spend watching Korean makeup tutorials on YouTube to sitting quietly and saying nice things *to* yourself about yourself. Set a timer for thirty seconds and compliment the sh*t out of yourself.

If you find that hard, I want you to play a somewhat devious but incredibly effective game. I call it "Just Kidding." Have you ever found yourself complaining about something, and then something far worse happens and you would suddenly give anything to have your old problem back? This happened to millions of people at the beginning of 2020. "Did I say I was over work travel?" "Did I complain about how hard it was to put this wedding together?" *Just kidding!*

When something is taken off the table, we realize how much there was to be grateful for, even in trying circumstances.

So…when I feel like I've had a tough week of long hours and too little sleep, and I feel like I am looking a little old, I will quickly take a picture of myself in my head and show it to myself twenty years from now. Guess what? Tracy in 2042 thinks I look AMAZING! So dewy! So vibrant! And I remember that even on the most superficial level, I have so much to be grateful for right now at this minute. A dear friend of mine always says, "I wish I was as skinny as I was when I thought I was fat." While the truth of this makes me giggle, it also breaks my heart because it reminds me that I have never truly appreciated my body at any point in my life.

This is where it gets a little dark, but bear with me because this is important. Think about a body part you don't like on yourself. Now think about how somebody out there has lost that part of themselves to cancer, an accident, or a genetic defect. They would give anything to have your legs, even with cellulite or varicose veins! They would give anything to have two working arms, batwing or not.

Anything about yourself that hampers your Self-Confidence is a gift. Remember that. Because, as much as you might hate your big ears, you would really miss them if they were gone.

I want you to go on a gratitude rampage RIGHT NOW. As psychotherapist Barry Michels and psychiatrist Phil Stutz say in their bestselling book *The Tools*, "Gratitude is the appreciation of things that are given to you...[by] a beneficent force that's interested in your welfare. Practicing it regularly allows you to master your own mind, which is the only thing you can really control anyway."

List all the things about yourself that you are grateful for. All the amazing parts of yourself that *do* something. Lungs that breathe, eyes that see, skin that clears toxins from your body, feet that get you from place to place, arms that carry your groceries and pick up your dog! You are a miracle.

Summing It Up

When I need to boost my Self-Confidence, I focus on all the things I can do for myself. For me, self-reliance has always made me feel incredibly good about myself. I can do my own bookkeeping for my business, generate a profit-and-loss sheet for my company, and even change the oil in my car. If I'm feeling low, fixing something, making something, or doing something by myself and for myself pumps me up to feeling proud of myself.

Never has this been more true than when I started growing my own vegetables. I started with the easy stuff… basil, tomatoes, and oregano—all foods that I love. Then I graduated to a full rainbow of vegetables. There is nothing like walking out into your yard or over to a window box and picking something for dinner. Talk about wellness!

First, I dramatically increased the amount of locally

sourced food I was eating. I wasn't bringing home vegetables in plastic bags. I reduced the carbon footprint of my meals to nearly zero. Best of all, every time I looked out my window at those green shoots, I brimmed with Self-Confidence. The kind that no one can sell to me.

Remember ad woman extraordinaire Georgina? After our walk, Georgina started volunteering at the Small Business Administration (SBA) in a mentorship program for young entrepreneurial women. And for exercise, she started a walking group with some old colleagues. They laughed about the old days and informed each other about new trends.

Most of all, she was grateful to finally have quieted the endless chatter in her mind about her appearance. Because your brain is your most valuable space—not your counter or closet or garage. When you allow these companies to undermine your confidence, you are giving away valuable mental real estate that could be put to much better use.

Think about that. What do you want to store in your uncluttered brain? A new language? A new skill? A new initiative at work or at home? The possibilities are endless. The space is yours.

4

magnetize free time

"No such thing as spare time, no such thing as free
time, no such things as down time. All you got is life
time. Go."

HENRY ROLLINS

MAGGIE AND I WENT TO COLLEGE TOGETHER, BUT
then our lives diverged. I went from acting to assisting to
organizing, and she went to law school. In some sense, she
was Miranda and I was Carrie, and my early days in LA
looked *nothing* like law school. We shared a passion for
structure and tackling paperwork. She worked insanely
hard, and while we saw each other less often because of her
demanding job, I was excited to see where she was going in

her career. Then, shortly into making partner at her firm, she became pregnant with her first child and decided to leave work. This is not an uncommon story for women in industries that don't allow mothers enough flexibility. When you are measured by billable hours, it's hard to reduce working time. She became an at-home mother of three. When the pandemic hit, she asked me to help her clear out her garage so she could turn it to an open-air workspace for her two older girls.

As we were catching up, it was clear that the lockdown was inflaming an already tense situation. "They treat me like a chauffeur, but if they need help with anything academic, they go to their dad. I have to remind them that I was summa cum laude—not their father."

"Don't they know what a rock star you were?" I asked.

She shrugged. "All they care about are TikTok influencers."

I opened a giant cardboard box filed with hundreds of mixtapes. "Oh my God," I exclaimed. "The tapes!" In college, Maggie had been famous for her mixtapes. She had spent hours and hours making them for friends and classmates.

"Yep," she said proudly. "I still have all of them. I *loved* making these. Oh, wait. Wow, with all their sports canceled, we can finally listen to them together. I've been waiting for this!"

"Do you still have a tape player?" I asked.

She thought for a second. "No."

"Well," I said. "Maybe we could digitize some of them?" Forget that the songs are all on Spotify, and she could just make playlists just like the kids do.

"Oh, that's a great idea!" she said enthusiastically.

Then we opened another box. More mixtapes.

And another.

And another.

My jaw dropped. She had moved countless times with literally thousands of tapes she could no longer even play.

"OK," I said. "Well, the great news is that we can haul most of these out of here and start setting up the girls' desks tomorrow."

"Wait," she said. "Are you suggesting getting rid of them?"

"Well, yes."

"No!" she said, aghast. "I can't get rid of these."

"Maggie! Why not?" I asked. She is an old friend, so we really got into it—back and forth, back and forth.

Finally, she said, "Because if I throw them away it's like admitting I wasted my time! All those hours!"

Time is something we all covet, and none of us feel like we ever have enough of it. But in the pursuit of more time or better-spent time, some people attract mountains of clutter that either validate the time they have already spent or promise more—and then take it instead.

This Clutter Magnet is about magnetizing Free Time. And looks at how too often we buy all kinds of gadgets, doodads, and unitaskers to save time, but these time-saving devices often end up becoming time-sucking clutter instead.

My clients manifest this Clutter Magnet in two ways. Some, like Maggie, are throwing good time after bad. They spend years doing something they aren't sure is a good use time, and then they can't bear to get rid of the fruits of their labor. They have three dozen bird houses. Stacks of knitted afghans. A giant Christmas village. Old projects taking up space, burning mental energy, and requiring care.

My other group keeps buying things that promise to save time. Kitchen gadgets. Workout gear. Storage equipment. Styling tools. These suck up time and energy. What these clients need is to be maintained and managed. We are going to examine both groups, but first, let's talk about the most potent commodity: time itself.

Time moves relentlessly in one direction and at a dizzying speed. Yet, in science fiction, we love to imagine that we can travel through it and change the course of our lives—that the inexorable march can be manipulated to our benefit.

On one level, time is the great equalizer because it can't be bought, and no one knows how much they have left. Being supremely wealthy certainly lengthens the *average* lifespan, but we don't know who will live to be a centenarian or who will be gone too soon. From James Dean to Heath Ledger, we are always stunned and heartbroken when a star dies young with so much of their brilliant potential unrealized. And we are reminded that all the success in the world cannot buy anyone more time. That can cause a lot of anxiety, whether we openly acknowledge it or not.

On another level, time is not as egalitarian as it may first seem. Why? Because time is measured in money. Whether or not we consciously realize it, we assign value to things and experiences based on how many hours we had to work to afford them. How many hours did it take to earn this salad, this sneaker, or this car? The less time it took, the less value it has. Sometimes I'll be on a high-profile job, and the client is giving away all their furniture from a house they lived in for only a year or two. They are moving on, and none of what they have fits their designer's vision for the new place. Or they are being relocated across the country. I will scramble to rehome their dining sets and sectionals to their employees, their neighbors, and their families, but relative to my client's income from, say, a multimillion-dollar professional sports contract, the five-thousand-dollar sofa is pretty expendable. For them, relative to my income, that sofa is equal to a latte.

On the flip side, think about that the next time you see college kids getting Starbucks or eating out at the next table. They are excited because relative to what they make at their work-study job or summer gig, that coffee or burger is a big deal; it took *time* to earn. They'd better enjoy it.

Your stuff costs you time.

Our *time* is the true global currency. It's what we trade for the money we earn. And then, too often, we next trade that money for clutter. On the simplest mathematical level, there is a clear equation here. Your stuff costs you time.

The question is: how much?

I do not only mean how much of your time are you exchanging for things you don't need, but how much are you trading away for what becomes clutter? Because every so-called time-saving device still needs to be stored, cleaned, and repaired. If these items are not benefiting you, then you are trading away your precious time twice over.

What Gets in the Way

Certain things in life certainly take more time than we want, and that time-suck empirically contributes to life dissatisfaction. Commuting is a great example. Studies have shown that adding twenty minutes to a daily commute makes a person as miserable as being dealt a 19-percent pay cut.[1] In fact, one of the things many people enjoyed during the beginning of the pandemic was the temporary end of commuting.

If we could buy something to give us back that time stuck in traffic or waiting at an airport, we all would. That would be valuable.

However, we cannot. Instead, we are suckers for so-called time-saving devices that usually do no such thing. Using a combined shampoo-conditioner for the last ten years has probably not helped you learn Mandarin with the minutes you saved, for example.

My clients with what I call "efficiency clutter," (which we can all agree wins the prize for most ironic Clutter Magnet) are trapped with excess goods they have bought in pursuit of getting time back. I always have to point out that they *spent* considerable time watching the ads, reading the reviews, trying the thing, mastering the thing, deciding the thing didn't deliver, finding a place for the thing, cleaning the thing, stepping over the thing, and being annoyed at themselves for going through it all in the first place.

Let's talk for a second about genuine time-savers. If you are someone like me who used to commute to a spinning class, you may also have discovered during the pandemic that an exercise bike gave you back an hour of your workday. That's real. For my clients with small children, bags of pre-chopped vegetables allow them to get a nutrient-rich dinner on the table quickly. If you were walking to the coffee shop several times a day, a countertop espresso machine might save you time *and* money. Being able to choose an assigned seat at the movie theater and roll up right as the previews start gives you more time to linger over dinner.

Nearly everything these days is marketed as a time-saving device, yet hardly any physical item you can buy actually does that. Here are things that do not save time: the Instant Pot. You first braise the meat, wait twenty minutes for the machine to reach pressure, and wait another twenty minutes for it to release pressure. The hands-off cooking time might have been compressed, but that is a LOT of waiting around, and this is why they are the first kitchen gadget my clients declutter.

Smart phones. Yes, they are an encyclopedia in our

pockets, and Siri can tell us which actor was in that thing with that other actor...BUT check your screen time for the last week. Make sure you are sitting down when you do because it's sure to be a shocker. According to the research marketing firm eMarketer, the average American adult spends three hours and forty-six minutes a day on their phone.[2] That works out to be fifty whole days each year! Maybe some of that is for genuinely useful pursuits, like reading the news, responding to emails, or finding the quickest route to a restaurant, but a lot of it is most likely mindless scrolling. Scrolling doesn't enrich our lives, and it leaves us vulnerable to all the overshopping we have been discussing. It is a double whammy of a time-sucking clutter portal!

My working parent clients are especially vulnerable to time-saver marketing because they are so crunched for time. This looks like a lot of purchased "systems" that never got implemented, but a system can only save time if it is up and running.

Lina, my client and a mother of three, did the thing where you buy each of your kids five backpacks—one for each day of the week—and then you are supposed to pack them all on Sunday night for the entire week. It sounds nice, doesn't it? The ballet tights, snack bars, and cleats already dispersed? It certainly made the rounds in all the parenting magazines.

> **A system can only save time**
> **if it is up and running.**

In reality, Lina was too tired on Sunday nights to pack the backpacks after track meets and homework wars for three children. Other times, she'd start and find stinky jerseys from the week before and suddenly need to start laundry, pulling her completely off course. Instead of kicking the week off with one less thing on every morning's to-do list, she now had FIFTEEN backpacks cluttering her mudroom and one more failed time-saving system.

I often think she would've done better with this system (and the other systems she tried and ultimately gave up on) if she had thought about them not as *saving* time but as *reallocating* time, which is more accurate. The bags have to be emptied, and the bags have to be filled. Unless you grow more hands, that takes the time it takes. It's simply a question of when—are you doing it all on Sunday night or as you go through the week? It's not going to go faster, but with a system in place, you may get out of having to do it first thing in the morning. *Maybe.*

Lina and I decided that it was worth giving it one more crack (she owned all the backpacks, after all), but this time on Saturday mornings, which was usually when her wife took the kids to soccer. After a good night's sleep and a full cup of coffee, she could empty and refill the bags while listening to a podcast. She found that that was a routine she could stick to.

Before you buy one more color-coded bin or bucket or another whiteboard or chore chart, here is what I will say: get honest about the time and effort it will take to get your new system up and running.

Then, please, I beg you, do not start with intentions like "After the baby goes to sleep, I'm going to…" No, you won't. You will fall asleep. Don't say, "I'll just set my alarm twenty minutes earlier…" No, you will sleep through it. Or maybe you won't. But only if you go to bed twenty minutes earlier. Can you realistically commit to that? Do not discount how much you need to sleep. A proper night's sleep is one of the best things you can do for your health. So don't throw the proverbial baby out with the bathwater and give up sleep *and* time.

Also, decide at the outset that you are going to commit to a new system for at least thirty days straight without judgment. What seems hard at first could become effortless within a month. It takes about that long for automaticity to kick in, for the routine to require no more effort than brushing your teeth. When we first got our dog, adding his walking routine to our packed schedules took real effort. Sometimes my partner and I would both be heading out the door and realize that neither of us had factored our boy into our day. Now, on the days that we just can't squeeze a walk in, I go to bed feeling like something is missing. So, remember, the system itself isn't magic. It won't polish your floors *Fantasia*-style, or pack the lunches. You have to invest in it to the point that it takes nothing from you to execute it—then you will reap the benefit.

Before you find yourself drowning in multicolored bento boxes, fridge buckets, or reusable snack bags, also ask yourself if this system will *actually* save time or if it will just create more clutter. Sometimes, even if a new system will be helpful, we just won't implement it. And that does not make you a bad person. It makes you realistic about your time and less apt to fall into the trap of the third Clutter Magnet.

You deserve to make life easier. But since the invention of Tupperware, women have been told that an easier life is on the other side of plunking down money on colored plastic when it might be on the other side of a tough conversation about who does what around the house.

As Eve Rodsky writes in her bestseller *Fair Play*, "Seventy-eight percent of moms say they are so busy maintaining family stability by being constantly available, mentally and physically, to deal with every detail of home life that they aren't taking care of themselves." Maybe reallocating roles and responsibilities in your household will give you back some of the time you crave.

One of my clients, Jeni, was experiencing tremendous friction in her marriage because of the household chores. The challenge was that her business paid 80 percent of the bills, but her husband Jordan's work as a photographer kept him traveling. Somehow over time, she had found that she was in charge of the financial stability of their family, she was the lead parent to their two girls, and she was responsible for all the household chores because she was at home seven days a week.

Gradually, the house got increasingly messier and more cluttered with his camera gear and home projects she couldn't find time to finish. He would arrive back from the airport annoyed at the state of the house, and she would fly into a rage because she didn't want to be judged when she felt like she was barely holding it all together.

Finally, she reached her breaking point. She realized that she had to take some of the household responsibilities off her plate beyond having someone come in to clean twice a month. She didn't want to give up her time with her kids or the enjoyable hands-on aspects of managing her household, like decorating for the holidays or helping her girls do DIY projects on their rooms. But she realized that some of the grunt work needed to go. In the end, she hired a personal assistant for ten hours a week.

This college student comes in and sorts the mail, returns packages to UPS, does all her household admin like soccer registration, runs all her errands, and frees her up to do the things she enjoys, like making dinner with her girls.

Now, her husband returns to a calmer home, which has incentivized him to put all his gear away and pitch in when he's there. Jeni realized that what had seemed like a luxury (an extra pair of hands and an extra brain) was a necessity for two working parents. It was worth it for her to trade some of the money she earned *back* for freed-up time by outsourcing some of the not-so-fun stuff on her plate.

Maybe instead of a system, you genuinely need more help. Virtual help. Admin help. Maybe a mother's helper, or an assistant share. But the answer to the time crunch might not be buying more stuff but hiring a living, breathing person to restore the calm. And without clutter.

Invariably, my clients who are obsessed with *saving* time are the ones who are worried about wasting time because they secretly (or not so secretly) are wasting it. Perhaps they have a job that they hate. Or wish they lived somewhere else. Or *with* someone else. They sense their one wild, precious life slipping away and rather than making the big, scary life changes, they buy pre-scrambled microwaveable egg mix. "Just heat and go!" They eat breakfast in their car, lunch at their desk, take calls during a haircut, and send work emails from the beach. It seems like they are squeezing the most out of every minute, but they are *missing nearly all of it*.

They have subsumed their anxiety into a mania for efficiency that is preventing them from enjoying—or confronting—the days of their lives.

On the clutter front, this can look like a lot of multiples. To be "efficient," people will order five of everything. They have a coffee maker in their office, their bedroom, and the kitchen. They found the new "it" pants and ordered ten pairs. They have several dopp kits and suitcases fully packed and ready to go. Where this goes haywire (because they're moving so fast) is when they forget what they already bought and order multiples on top of multiples, which they still have to organize, dry-clean, pack, and re-pack. These are the people who have drawers of mini shampoo bottles they've taken from hotels and never remembered to re-use.

Unsurprisingly, despite all their so-called time-saving purchases, what they still feel is panicked and pressed for time.

Even though I'm called in to streamline capsule wardrobes and conflicting coffee pods, I end up recommending one of the best time savers for these people, which is just *being present.*

It's simple, but not easy.

As Dr. Laurie Santos, a Yale professor who teaches a course called the Science of Happiness, says, "Happier people prioritize having a little more time."

Being present won't help you do anything faster, but it will help you enjoy and savor the time you do have. I tell these clients, "Don't drink your coffee in your car while listening to the news and dictating emails. Have at least one cup in the yard, by the window, or sitting on your fire escape. Look *out.* Taste your coffee. Taste your breakfast. Listen. Can you hear birds? Children? A dog? Take a deep breath. Be here."

Because there is no finish line. There is no prize for cramming in the most unenjoyed experiences. Time isn't the reward at the end of it all. In fact, you are spending it right now.

I have a client, Katie, who went to Yale. Right out of college, many of her friends went to work in junior analyst programs at big investment banks. At first, Katie was jealous. She was pursuing a writing career, which meant waiting tables at night, while these friends had real starting salaries. But their lifestyles were brutal. They went into the office seven days a week, and sleeping under their desks was not uncommon. One girl did the calculation and figured out she was actually making less than minimum wage when she broke it down per hour. In their fleeting Free Time, they went shopping at high-end stores to buy the things that could make them feel like they had achieved success.

When a drip of water from scaffolding fell on that girl's Prada bag and stained it, she sobbed like the world had ended. What was really ending was a career path that she had thought she'd wanted to pursue.

If you are trading away your Free Time for a job or lifestyle that doesn't fulfill or excite you, one that leads you to overbuy or overspend in order to surround yourself with items that can tell you the constant surge of cortisol pumping through your veins is worth it, it isn't.

How to Feel More Infinite

Time management is more or less behavior management because, unless you're an Avenger, time cannot be managed. Only behavior can be modified. I have a client, Emma, who was chronically late for everything, which made her scattered, and being scattered led to a lot of overshopping. Whenever she would arrive at her destination without what she needed, she'd re-buy it. But in a time-crunched panic, whatever she was grabbing was always just good enough to get her through the meeting, the dinner, or the trip, but it wasn't perfect. Then, when she'd get home, the item would get crammed into a drawer or shoved on an overcrowded shelf, never to be used or worn again.

Emma finally had her come-to-Jesus moment when she missed the curtain going up on a show she had really wanted to see and the ushers wouldn't let her in. She was alone, and she'd come from home. She had no husband or kids to blame for her departure time, no restaurant that had delayed getting her the check. She sat down on the sidewalk and cried until she realized that, somehow, she had let this thing that was already hers—her own Free Time—get out of her control.

She could take that control back.

All she had to do was assess how long each step of her day actually took, so she started timing herself. Eleven minutes to shower, six minutes to get dressed, and three for makeup. She could now work backward from the time she needed to leave the house and truly understand what time she needed to start getting ready. Then, she timed her work on a project and figured out exactly how many hours it took to complete one. Finally, she could make accurate projections at work that wouldn't leave her cramming overnight to meet her deliverables.

The other area where she had to get honest with herself was that she was overly optimistic about what she could get done in a certain amount of time. She was always trying to make one more call, send one more email, or do the dishes before she went out the door when she thought she had a few more minutes to spare. Using up those "spare" minutes for a small task compounded her habitual tardiness and stressed her out.

As her day-to-day life started to feel calmer, she realized that she had been unconsciously creating a lot of chaos to avoid thinking about shifts she needed to make in her life and work. She wanted to have a child, and it was increasingly clear that her husband at the time wasn't the person to start a family with. The next couple of years brought about upheavals, but she was able to breathe through each one because she showed up at every mediation on time and with all her paperwork, feeling calm and confident. She stopped needing to make emergency purchases, and she stopped creating emergencies.

Today, she is happily remarried with a little girl. She tells me, "Career and motherhood? *This* is the real crunch. I'm so glad I made myself a time boss when I did."

Our final obvious but most important lesson is…you can't get time back.

You can put every pair of baby shoes your child ever wore on velvet pillows in Lucite boxes under custom spotlights, but your children will still have grown up. You can spend thousands of dollars on a custom-made, photographer-curated shagreen photo album of your wedding and a giant dry-cleaner box for your dress, but the wedding is still just a party that happened sometime in the past. You can bring home every tchotchke from every stall in every city, but the vacation will still be over.

> **You can't get time back by cramming your home with mementos.**

I know that seems obvious, but so many of my clients fill their homes with unnecessary mementos to preserve something that can be remembered but never re-experienced. They are constantly magnetizing clutter in hopes of freezing time with the perfect set of photo frames, like with a fabric-covered box that holds every card anyone has ever sent them or the dreaded off-site storage unit that holds evidence of all their past endeavors.

Many of us need to make peace with how fleeting time is. Not to bum ourselves out, but to enjoy the moment for the sake of enjoying the moment. In our "pics or it didn't happen" culture, we've become so focused on capturing the moment that we often forget to *live* the moment. Have you been in a museum in the last few years and watched everyone move from piece to piece, snapping away without looking directly at anything right in front of them? And all of that art is digitized now anyway! We used to travel thousands of miles for the privilege of standing in front of the real thing, the real work of art the artist actually touched and made with their own hands. But somehow that has been lost. We also used to take a picture to have a reminder of an experience. Now, too often taking the picture *is* the experience.

On the opposite end of the spectrum, sometimes we have put a lot of time and energy into something that ended up being painful—perhaps a lackluster relationship or failed business. And we want all our invested hours to have added up to something.

I have wonderful news: they did. The experience.

The scratchy truth of existence is that we learn more from pain than pleasure. It's just how we're wired. It's the pain that makes us slow down and pay attention. It's the pain that prompts us to grow. You might not get the outcome you initially envisioned, but you'll have learned some really valuable lessons. If you are willing to sift through the whole experience without judgment, you will see that you have developed and changed, and you will take those lessons with you moving forward.

We're so success-oriented that we often have a hard time letting go. But even if a venture or adventure wasn't a success, it was still worth the time investment. It was still valuable. Remember Maggie and her mixtapes? In college, she enjoyed spending hours putting the tapes together. It was her creative outlet. Even though technology has changed and the tapes themselves are no longer useful, it was enough for her teenage self to spend time curating the music she loved.

I ask clients needing to hold on to the evidence of their past time spent, "Could you see the value of the *experience* without keeping the things themselves?" Memories are valuable. Just like souvenirs that catch dust, can the doing be enough without the having?

If you can validate *for yourself* that it was time well spent, you can release the items and free yourself up to fully inhabit the present.

Summing It Up

Once we got rid of all the boxes, Maggie realized that it wasn't the tapes she was worried she had wasted, but the years she had spent earning a degree, making partner at a law firm, and then choosing to be a mom who didn't work outside the home. She once loved being at home with her girls when they were little, but now that school and sports were their focus, staying home was becoming increasingly unfulfilling; she had basically become a chauffeur.

She knew she didn't want to go back to a seventy-hour work week, but also realized that there were a lot of places she could volunteer her legal skills. Once schools reopened and after-school activities resumed, she paired up with another family to carpool so she could have two full days a week to volunteer at an organization that aids families facing eviction. And the young man in IT at the nonprofit taught her how to make a Spotify playlist so she can relive her mixtapes whenever she wants—much to her coworker's chagrin.

Best of all, by looking at her Clutter Magnet and trying to make peace with how she spends her Free Time, she found fulfillment along the way, which we'll be looking at in Chapter Seven. Often times, when you heal one Clutter Magnet, more come along for the ride. It's called growing, and I don't ever want you to stop doing it.

5

magnetize big love

"Money can buy you a fine dog, but only love can make him wag his tail."

KINKY FRIEDMAN

WHEN I MET HEATHER, HER MARRIAGE WAS IN trouble. The source of the friction? An enormous $600-a-month storage bill for her late mother's personal effects. Her husband could not understand, when they were supposed to be saving up for a house to start a family, why Heather was spending their down payment to store the possessions of a woman with whom she'd had a terrible relationship. That toxic history was infecting her present-day partnership. She and her husband were fighting all the time about the storage units, but of course, the root of the thing is never the thing itself. Sure, the storage units were a huge financial drain, but the literal baggage Heather was paying for was building a wall between them. Her husband began to worry that maybe she didn't really want children and that their goals in life were irreconcilable.

Desperate to save her marriage, Heather called me to help empty the storage units. Having done this countless times with people, I know that letting go of the personal effects of a family member can be painful. Sometimes it feels like we are losing the person all over again. But what I have observed is that this process is challenging when we are in mourning for the loss of someone special to us, and when there are unresolved issues. When the relationship didn't meet our needs and now never can. That can be a very painful pill to swallow, and sometimes people want to avoid having to confront that reality. But Heather's avoidance was costing her.

When we arrived at the facility, I expected to find the contents of Heather's mother's little ranch house filling the two units with her clothes, furniture, and housewares. Instead, what Heather had packed up and stored were boxes and boxes of Hallmark Precious Moments figurines. "I don't know what to do with these," she said. "I don't want them, but I know they're so valuable. I know she wanted me to keep them, but we don't have the space. And if I don't sell them, we will never have the space because I'm spending our down payment on this storage. Can you help me list them for sale?"

"Heather," I said as I picked up my phone and tapped the eBay icon, deciding it could be the bearer of the bad news, "Right now, there are 80,378 results for Precious Moments on eBay."

"Really?" she said. "That means they're popular, right?"

"No," I said gently. "That means that a lot of people like you have inherited them and don't want them. It doesn't seem like anyone does because the average asking price is just a couple of bucks. No one is buying these things."

She looked absolutely sucker punched. "You're kidding. My mom always said this was a valuable collection. I told my husband we could afford to store them because I'd make the money back later." Heather was shaking her head and blinking back tears. I got the impression that it wasn't just that she'd been spending a fortune to store these worthless tchotchkes and that something else was wrong.

"Important to her maybe," I said rubbing her back as she doubled over, trying to breathe. "And that's valid. But that doesn't mean they need to be important to you."

"But I have to do *something* with them," she said miserably.

"Why?" I asked.

She fully started to cry. "Because she only cared about these stupid figurines! She never loved anyone or anything else." Oh. They were her *siblings*. The ones that got all her mother's attention and affection. I have seen this too often as well. The parent who lavished all their kindness on their dogs or their vintage cars or their clock collection. I call it the "Candice Bergen syndrome" after the ventriloquist dummy that the actress felt she had played second fiddle to her whole childhood.

Heather was paying to store figurines that she didn't even like because she was trying to find some sense of connection to her late mother. She was trying to fill the hole that the lack of love had left in her. The irony was that by trying to re-create that lost love, she was missing the love that was right in front of her from her husband and the family they wanted to create. No wonder he was angry and she was in turmoil.

Welcome to the chapter where we look at the never-simple, always-fraught relationship between having excess stuff and love—craving it, missing it, denying it. All these complex emotions can be found buried in any of my clients' overstuffed closets. This Clutter Magnet is a doozy when we realize we've been trying to fill a heart shaped hole with stuff, stuff, and more stuff.

As you can see from Heather, this Clutter Magnet does not just apply to romantic love, although I certainly know that pursuit is in play when I see rows of unworn date outfits, matching five-piece poolside ensembles bought for an unplanned getaway invitation, or unused golf clubs that were supposed to be an in with a new romantic interest.

We are also going to look at all the ways I see people shopping and acquiring as a means to soothe emotional pain. We're going to explore all the ways this can manifest, and then I'm going to walk you through shifting away from clutter and onto real love, big love.

Everyone wants to feel loved. Yet for some people, it's easier to attract piles of stand-ins than the feeling itself. I have clients who magnetize clutter and that keeps them from opening their homes to friends or potential partners. I have clients who spend their money and time collecting instead of connecting.

Don't collect—connect!

Some clients pour their time and energy in getting parts of their homes "just perfect" before they'll let themselves get the dog, the baby, or the boyfriend. Perfection is an ever-moving target that they can use to avoid the thing they crave (and fear) the most.

The work of this chapter is an uncomfortable roll-up-your-sleeves tussle with the relationship between love and stuff. (And how we stuff down our craving for love.) It can be uncomfortable because it's hard to admit that we're carrying those feelings if they are currently unmet or were unmet in the past by the people like caregivers, who should have made us feel unconditionally loved.

The process of getting honest with ourselves is the key to shifting our giant heart magnet from clutter to Big Love.

What Gets in the Way

Why is it so common to misdirect a desire for love onto shopping, collecting, or rummaging? Because our sense of whether or not we are loved feels very out of our control. We could have had parents or caregivers who were misattuned, which is the scientific way of saying not keyed into their baby's needs, for whatever reason—perhaps due to their own childhood experiences of trauma or neglect, addiction, financial necessity, or systemic racism.

One of my clients, Patty, spent long hours after school alone in a small apartment starting at the age of five. Her father drove a cab, and her mom was a waitress. She knows her parents did the best they could, but she grew up needing to surround herself with material security to avoid feeling lonely.

Of course, the endless money Patty spent on home design and renovation as an adult put her in a very financially precarious situation. She used the endless project of her home as an excuse to put off meeting anyone. She'd often say to me, "I can't have anyone over to the construction site!" Or "The dining table I really want is on backorder. Once it comes, I'll start hosting dinner parties!" It would come six months later, and she wouldn't like it and she'd return it, and the cycle would start all over again. It wasn't until we started really looking at her patterns that she saw that, under the rugs and custom upholstery, she was still that five-year-old girl waiting for the key to turn in the lock. She thought she had come so far by toiling hard to have her dream home. But as we started working together, she realized that her dream home was really one that was filled with people she loved.

Unfortunately, that is so often how the progression manifests. A lack of emotional security in childhood doesn't set us up to be the best intimacy-finders in adulthood. So, the lack of love compounds over the years and doesn't improve.

That's part of why this process can be thorny— underneath an unsatisfying situation frequently sits an old wound that is desperate to heal, not merely to be soothed. Instead of healing, what my clients have been doing, some- times for years, is transferring the desire for Big Love to shopping. We can often be glib about it—*Oh, right, sure, retail therapy!*—but if we slow down and pay attention to what's happening in our mind and body, we will be better able to catch ourselves in the future.

A word about the phrase "retail therapy." I'm sure you can imagine how often I hear it, and how it makes me want to gnash my teeth to powder when I am helping a client dig out from under the consequences. I'm not denying that shopping will make you feel better for a few minutes, but it isn't therapy. Or even therapeutic. It's a treat. If you call it that, then you have to ask yourself…is this a treat I can afford? Just like treating yourself to a hot fudge sundae or a second margarita. If this an occasional indulgence, then it really is a treat. If this is something you find you are doing regularly, then it's a habit, and it's one with side effects like weight gain, hangovers, or clutter. Starting to use language that pushes us to get honest about our habits is where real change comes from.

When you feel that impulse for mall therapy, slow down and notice what is happening.

First, there is the trigger.

It could be something from the past, like a loss. Maybe the anniversary of your mother's death is approaching. Or you just found out that your ex is remarrying.

Or it could be something very much in the present. An unfulfilling conversation with a parent who doesn't even ask you how you are or who offers unsolicited criticism. Maybe it's a boss or colleague who isn't acknowledging your contribution or has a habit of undermining you. Maybe it's an actual romantic snub—an unreturned text or a second date that is failing to materialize.

The feelings those experiences can create are uncomfortable. Shame, grief, self-loathing, rejection—none of it is anything we are naturally good at sitting with, so we opt to distract ourselves.

We scroll on our phones or grab our car keys and hit the shops. We don't even know what we want exactly except to feel better. We look at pretty things that we think will give us a pretty life. *The person who owns these fancy towels doesn't ever feel like this. They have all the love they crave in their lives.* And then we pick something we don't need and don't even really like. We click purchase or take a bunch of stuff to the checkout.

And we feel great! Euphoric, even.

That feeling may last all the way through the parking lot, bags swinging. If we're lucky, it take us all the way home. Excited, we put out the new towels or clear space for the new shoes. And for a few minutes, everything feels brighter.

There is a voice in our heads that says, "See! I can control how I feel. I used my adult powers to go out and change something about my life." But within hours, those towels are just towels, the shoes aren't as comfortable as you thought, or you've spilled something on the blouse. In the meantime, we have done nothing to address the core issue of the hurt and how we respond to those events. We still don't have the Big Love we were looking for, no matter how many shopping bags we fill.

What we need to focus our time and energy on instead is learning how to sit with those uncomfortable, yucky feelings and process them. Without shopping. For me, when those feelings bubble up, I think about my nieces and nephew, and the love that flows between us. Their warm little hands on my arm when I read them a story. Their belly laughs when I tell a bad joke. Or driving with my oldest niece and sharing a piece of music we think the other will love.

If that doesn't do the trick, I can always count on my dog to remind me that I am loved and needed. If the place you live doesn't allow animals, local shelters always need volunteer belly-rubbers. Local foster agencies always need people to take rescued animals for a few days or weeks until they can find their forever homes.

Even without thinking about loving people or pets, we can make a shift inside of ourselves. I have one client who started walking around the block each time she felt slighted by her family or her colleagues. Just getting up and moving while consciously saying to herself, "I am moving these feelings through me with every step I take," created a new habit.

After a couple of months, she stopped reflexively shopping on her iPad every time she felt triggered. What she was surprised to discover was that there were a host of unintended benefits to her new walking habit. First off, her credit card debt halved. That made her feel really good about herself. Second, she didn't have to work so hard to keep her home tidy because she wasn't constantly cluttering it with new things. That increased her sense of serenity. Both benefits gave her a *real* sense of control instead of the fleeting one she used to get shopping online.

In our last session, she said to me, "Tracy, I am finding that I love myself more. And I love my life more. I didn't realize that trying to make myself feel better was actually making me feel worse in the long run."

Let's take a minute and think of all the things you can do instead of shopping when your love tank is low. You could call an old friend and check in. They would be so happy to hear from you, and they will ooze love for you. Write a postcard to someone you love, just to say you're thinking of them. Call the old gang and plan a reunion. Tell everyone to bring their favorite story about the group to share at the event. The possibilities are endless, but do you notice what all these activities have in common? They are not rooted in acquiring stuff. Remember, stuff does not love us back. People (and pets) do!

Another group working through unresolved child-hood wounds via stuff are the people buying and collecting things that remind them of their childhood. That sounds cute, doesn't it? Let me unpack that for you. They aren't filling their houses with their own McDonald's The Great Muppet Caper Glasses from 1981. They are filling their houses with *someone else's*! Someone else had the presence of mind to realize that they no longer needed twelve Miss Piggy cups, and my client went out and snatched up every last one. They are going out, buying a Holly Hobbie lunch box—or an Easy-Bake Oven or an Etch A Sketch that someone else played with forty years ago—and bringing it home to remind them of…what, exactly?

I have yet to meet a client who collects these things and who also did not have a troubled childhood. The story typically goes like this: "Well, we moved around a lot, so I was never allowed to have X, Y, or Z." Or "After my mom remarried the fourth time, we had to give everything away, and I never found out where my Cabbage Patch Kids dolls went." Or "My little brother always got whatever he asked for, but I was never allowed to have these toys. I don't know why." What they *really* want to do is go back in time and find security—the "core sense of love and belonging," as Brené Brown puts it—that was absent. They try to fill that sense of emptiness with the actual objects, but it's not as if they will make a Rainbow Brite picture in their midforties and suddenly feel better.

This pattern could also be a sign of unresolved trauma. Trauma is an often misunderstood term that people are reluctant to associate with their own life events. Childhood trauma is any event the child's brain finds too overwhelming to process, compounded by the absence of an attuned adult to help them. These events don't have to look like things our adult perspectives deem traumatic, like a car accident or an incarcerated parent. They can be the little traumas, like being humiliated at school, moving, or losing a beloved grandparent. Without an adult to help the child through these challenges, they can feel overwhelming—and that feeling can stay with us for years.

In the Appendix is a short quiz developed by the Centers for Disease Control and Prevention (CDC) to help people measure their adverse childhood experiences, or ACES, score.

This could be helpful information for you to have as you move through the work of separating your feelings from the stuff you surround yourself with. If your score is high, that is useful to take stock of and maybe even bring into therapy.

I have a client I call Sad Cher. Just like in *Clueless*, she was raised in Beverly Hills by a wealthy widower. But, unlike Cher, she was completely neglected. She went to the University of California San Diego (UCSD) and became a big party girl, developing a serious pill problem and shopping problem along the way.

Without the benefit of therapy, she married a man just like her father—successful, but wholly absent. Her adulthood mirrored the childhood she'd been so desperate to escape, wandering around alone in a giant house with no one who really cared about her. To cope, she became the MVP of clothes shopping. And she never wore *any* of it. She was constantly testing the limits of what would be the purchase to get her husband and father to notice her. Once, I was getting lunch with her at Whole Foods, and her debit card was declined. I offered to pay and she said, "No, watch this." From the line she called American Express and had a cash advance transferred from her dad's credit card into her checking account. "Well, that will get his attention," she said as they rung up our salads.

That was my aha moment.

I brought her back to her house to finish going through all her unpacked purchases bag by bag. I held up each item, and instead of asking her if she wanted to keep, or donate, or resell, I said, "This shirt did not make you feel better. This bag did not make you feel better. These pants, this sweater, and these earrings did not make you feel better. None of these things can make you feel loved. You are deep in the Clutter Magnet of trying to magnetize the feeling of Big Love through stuff."

At first, she thought it was funny. Then she got annoyed, and finally, she was sobbing. I said, "I am driving you right now to a Debtors Anonymous meeting. Obviously, you're not broke. But you need a system and a structure to hold you accountable to not shop while you finally allow these feelings of neglect to come up and be processed."

It can be hard for some people to see that they have a truly addictive relationship with shopping, one that they use to avoid a host of painful feelings. Having a supportive community of people taking an honest look can help us see that shopping will only provide a quick fix, while what we are really after, always, is Big Love. Love, love, and more love!

Sad Cher was initially enormously reluctant to look harder at her shopping, but she also knew that her coping strategy wasn't serving her anymore, if it ever had. As

Chelsea Handler said on the *Smart Less* podcast when discussing how the loss of her brother at nine years old caught up with her in her forties, "Everything works for you until it doesn't. In my case it was my anger. [I realized] Oh, I need to get some help here, I'm not doing great anymore. And what was working for me before isn't working for me now."

Unproductive coping strategies—like overeating, overshopping, drinking excessively, or even exercising excessively—will catch up with us and become problems. By putting herself into a supportive community, Sad Cher was able to create more authentic connections and take control of her behavior. Once she stopped shopping to fill her days and started to heal her wounds, she found that her husband was much more present with her. They were able to do the hard work for their marriage to figure out if it was a Big Love worth saving. It was not easy, but as she said to me months later, "Some of the stuff I'm looking at now is really painful. But I'm realizing that it was always there, just under the surface of all the distractions. I was always in pain, I was just running from it. But you can't outrun what's inside you—even if you buy thirty-seven pairs of sneakers."

We laughed, and I was glad to see her gaining these insights.

Sometimes it's not the siren song of the stuff that calls

us, but the activity of shopping itself. One way people use shopping to create false connections is through excessive gift giving. I have many clients who are constantly buying gifts. I mean, constantly. When no one they know has a birthday, anniversary, or graduation, they stockpile gifts "just to have on hand." Baby clothes, candles, nice pens, tote bags. But when everything could be a present for an imaginary someone or self-proclaimed holiday of importance, nothing is off limits. This might be one of the hardest stealth shopping addictions to break. Buying gifts for other people *feels* altruistic, but under the veneer of selflessness and generosity, there's a gaping maw of need.

I have learned over the years that, in this case, the person giving the gift needs to give it more than the recipient needs to get it. These receivers of the gifts don't end up feeling showered with affection. They feel used because they know that their parent, or aunt, or in-law has a shopping addiction and is just using that purchase to get their fix. One of my clients, Kitsi, kept receiving knickknacks from her mother-in-law that she didn't need or want, including an incredibly heavy monogrammed sterling silver purse mirror. It was expensive and impractical in every way. Finally, I encouraged Kitsi to reach out to her mother-in-law and see if they could come up with a shared activity that they could do a few times a year in lieu of gift giving. I thought that maybe it would help give her mother-in-law the sense of connection that she was clearly craving without the clutter. And trust me, there are no happier words a mother-in-law wants to hear than, "Let's hang out."

Now they go on a wine tasting afternoon a few times a year, and through that process, they have become genuinely close in ways Kitsi never imagined possible.

Whether it's a shopping addiction fix or a codependent fix like we discussed earlier, if the gift is all about the giver and not the recipient, it doesn't accomplish its goal. No one walks away from the interaction feeling loved. And if the receivers don't speak up and point out the problem, they become enablers. By accepting the continuous gifts, they are sending a message to the buyer that reinforces the Clutter Magnet.

> **If the gift is all about the giver**
> **and not the recipient,**
> **no one walks away from the**
> **interaction feeling loved.**

I tell these clients, "You can make one last purchase. Note cards. Moving forward every person you used to buy gifts for will get flowers, chocolate, or wine accompanied by a handwritten note expressing your fullest, most genuine feelings. I promise you this is something they will cherish much longer and more thoroughly than a decanter."

Dr. Laurie Santos, the Yale professor I mentioned earlier, who teaches a free course called the Science of Happiness, sites a study showing that writing a handwritten thank you note raises dopamine levels for the sender for a full month following the activity.[1] And we all know how good receiving a heartfelt thank you feels! Try incorporating longhand gratitude into your life! This strategy helps these clients break the habit of constantly combing retail shelves or turning every occasion into an acquisition crisis.

It does free up some time in their lives too, which can be scary. I always have to ask, "You made gift giving into a big activity for yourself. What are you going to do with that wonderful, precious time now?"

There is always a period of adjustment, but inevitably these clients use their time to address whatever it was that they were trying to ignore by shopping. Sometimes that means making a big life adjustment or starting a therapeutic exploration. But on the other side is a life where they are not trying to buy Big Love and instead are genuinely giving and receiving it.

How to Break the Cycle

Clearly, this Clutter Magnet encompasses some of the most tenacious emotional shopping habits. I have seen clients accomplish huge shifts just by becoming aware of the connection between what's missing in their emotional life and their shopping habits. That's where we can start.

The first step to breaking these habits is to slow down the reactive cycle between the impulse to buy and the actual purchase, so you have time to ask yourself some valuable questions. Cultivating a simple meditation practice, even just ten minutes a day of sitting quietly, can help with that. Meditation teaches our brain how to increase the gap between emotion and reaction. We learn that we don't need to instantly discharge every uncomfortable feeling. That makes the space we need—even if it's just a few minutes. You'll be surprised to see how simple a meditation practice is, and what a sense of peace it will bring.

If you don't know where to start, check out the Waking Up app, which offers a commitment-free trial for thirty days. Sam Harris, the creator, is a neuroscientist, philosopher, and best-selling author. He has done much research into the benefits of meditation, and he created this easy-to-use app to make meditation accessible to anyone with a smartphone. As an aside, it has really worked for me.

If scrolling your feed for targeted ads is how you like to

numb uncomfortable emotions like rejection or loneliness, and if you routinely find yourself mesmerized like Mowgli by the python in *The Jungle Book*, then pause, take a breath, and say out loud, "OK, I'm looking at these ads. How am I feeling right now? Can I put the phone down and check in with myself?"

Close your eyes for a few seconds. Did something happen today that your brain is trying to distract you from? Can you name it?

I might say out loud, "It felt ouchy this morning when _____." And then I breathe into it. Which is always when I realize that I've been holding my stomach in for several hours. In many yogic traditions, our solar plexus, right below where our rib cage ends, is considered the seat of identity and our sense of self. When our sense of self takes a hit, it's normal to clench that area out of self-protection. But it also makes it hard to take those big breaths we really need. Once I am able to get some oxygen to all the parts of me that were bracing against the feeling, I allow the feeling in. Am I sad? Am I angry? All feelings are welcome. It's running from the feelings that has magnetized all this clutter.

Consider this. If this is a small hurt, allow for the possibility that the other person was wrapped up in their own thing and that none of it had anything to do with you. So often that turns out to be true, doesn't it?

If this feeling is the echo of a deep wound, allow it in. Allow the hurt, and allow the truth of your unmet needs. Some small part of you is hurting. Respect that, and don't try to soothe it with a purchase.

After that, I figure out how I'm going to move this feeling through me. I usually take my dog and my fella out for a walk. But you don't need to have a dog to stretch your legs—you can just head out on your own. What can you notice while you're out? The trees? Your neighbor's flowers? Studies have shown that just looking at nature makes us feel better.[2]

This is also the perfect moment to focus on gratitude. Sometimes clients say to me, "But how can I be grateful for what I have now when I'm still in so much pain over what I didn't get then?" That is exactly the root of the gratitude.

You can simply feel gratitude for your child self who survived and got you here. Gratitude for your parents, who did the best they could with the tools they had. Gratitude for the life that you built and the love that you have. Gratitude for everything you are and are capable of. Because when you focus on all that you *have*, it moves your attention off what you *want* and gives you time and space to quiet the shopping impulse.

As Dr. Robert Emmons of the University of California, Davis said on NPR, "We know from studies that gratitude helps us recover from loss and trauma. It helps us to deal with the slow drip of everyday stress as well as the massive personal upheavals in the face of suffering and pain and loss, and trials and tribulations. Gratitude is absolutely essential. It's part of our psychological immune system."

I *love* that.

Summing It Up

There is nothing more painful than feeling a lack of love in our lives. But stuff doesn't love us back, no matter how much we wish it would or what we imbue it with. Remember Heather in the storage unit? Well, she was still seeking her mother's love and approval by holding on to her figurines— and putting her own marriage in jeopardy in the process. For her, healing meant truly accepting and mourning that she was never going to get the love from her mother that she had always wanted and deserved.

However, once she accepted that and did the work to mourn what she had been denied, she was able to unload the storage units, and demonstrate a commitment to the future with her husband. Today she has the family she craved her whole life, filled with actual precious moments—the kind you live out and not the kind you dust. And as Oprah has wisely been heard to say numerous times: "Forgiveness is giving up the hope that the past could have been any different, it's accepting the past for what it was, and using this moment and this time to help yourself move forward."[3]

Instead of trying to feel love from an object, remember that you can have a satisfying, loving relationship with yourself. In fact, truly the most important person who needs to love you is you. And you are in control of that! You can shower yourself with love all the time and in so many ways. None of which involve shopping. In fact, I would argue that a habit of self-soothing through shopping undermines self-love. And if you are feeling good and corny, sing along to Whitney Houston's "Greatest Love of All."

The next time you want to treat yourself, get a massage, buy some flowers, take yourself out for a nice meal, give yourself a huge hug, or take a moment to say to the one and only you: "I love you just as you are."

You will be amazed at what comes flowing into your life from there.

6

magnetize self-respect

"Character—the willingness to accept responsibility for one's own life—is the source from which self-respect springs."

JOAN DIDION

A CLIENT IN HER FIFTIES, NINA, HAD LEFT HER LAW firm to start her own practice and called me in to help her set up the new office because, as she put it, "Once I unpacked, it looked like a dusty old law library threw up in here. I haven't even been here a week, and I managed to make this place look horribly dated. None of this is the image I want to project."

When I arrived, the office did indeed look like she had been there for years. Every inch of the walls was covered in laminated prints of Nina's press coverage, ugly old Lucite awards, and photos of her sporting '90s-era tawny lipstick and thin eyebrows while smiling with celebrities. The bookcases were crammed with giant sets of leather-bound books and stacks upon stacks of clippings and legal pads. None of it felt fresh.

"When you look around this room," I asked, "how does all this clutter make you feel?"

She took a deep breath and considered. "Respected."

I asked a follow-up question that you can probably predict at this point. "Could you feel respected without any of this?"

She immediately teared up. "So, the thing is, *both* my parents were lawyers. Serious corporate lawyers, not *entertainment* lawyers." She rolled her eyes at her own profession. "And I always felt like anything I accomplished just wasn't enough. Anything I did, my mom had done first—and better. I think I started collecting all of this law paraphernalia just to prove that I can do my job."

"But now you are a highly respected and sought-after lawyer," I said. "Could you believe that in an empty room?"

She took a deep breath. "Maybe?"

"If anything, all this old stuff makes it look like you haven't done anything recently. It's actually counterproductive to whatever you are trying to project."

"OK, let's do this," she said. "Let me get all the boxes back."

Once we cleared out all the memorabilia, her office felt fresh, modern, and stylish. And she went on to build a thriving solo practice that brought her a renewed amount of press attention, but no one ever asked for a press kit. Her reputation was enough.

When it comes to the Clutter Magnet of magnetizing Self-Respect, so many of my clients magnetize status clutter. It's not just watches and cars or Birkin bags and jewelry—it's every award they ever received or every client gift they should have tossed or donated. I have clients at various socioeconomic levels who need to have a logo on *all* of their clothes and accessories. Whether it's Gucci or Michael Kors or bebe, there are letters swirling all over their bodies. And I ask them, "Are you afraid that no one will know that you are successful if you don't announce your purchase power?"

Having more stuff—or nicer stuff—does not fill you with Self-Respect. Trust me, I know. I work with people every week who have lots of beautiful stuff, and they are not any happier than anyone else. Their possessions have not made them immune to divorce, disappointment, loss, or aging.

One afternoon, I was called in to do a big closet renovation for one of my biggest clients. This woman is not only hugely famous, but she is also hugely talented and is a creative businessperson as well. She is the real deal—a person with rare skills who works hard at employing them. Needless to say, this is someone I have enormous respect for. I had done a few projects for her in the past, setting up other homes and helping with moves, but somehow, I had never crossed paths with her personal closet.

I went into her dressing room that day with the architect and assistant to strategize how the room would be redone and what could be given away. What we found floored me. It wasn't the floor-to-ceiling shelves of shoes, bags, and gowns—that is all in a day's work for me and doesn't faze me anymore. It was the knockoffs. Hundreds of fake designer watches and purses in the closet of a woman who could more than afford the real things.

I stood there, holding a very light Rolex in one hand and a pleather Gucci in the other and thought, "Huh, didn't see this coming." Why would you only buy bags and clothes with obvious logos to show that you could afford them—and when you could clearly afford them—but not let yourself have the authentic items? Talk about impostor syndrome.

When I asked the client about it months later, she admitted, "When I came to LA, I was so broke for so long, and I was trying to make a good impression. Part of me knows this can all go away tomorrow, so I'd better not spend my money foolishly. And part of me still thinks I have to prove myself to everyone by donning these brands. So, I found a way to split the difference. As I'm saying it out loud, I hear how crazy it is." Because none of it was coming from a place of Self-Respect. If she carried around the respect for her innate talents and amazing work ethic (both of which would ensure a long and fruitful career) instead of the knockoff purse, she would feel calm and secure no matter what.

Despite being one of the biggest and hardest working stars on the planet, it didn't occur to her that she could feel confident about her abilities or her success without flashing designer logos. Is it any wonder I work with so many women who have come to rely on brand names for their confidence, instead of loving fashion for the art of it?

What Gets in the Way

Depending on how old you are, you may not even remember the world before it was packed with status symbols. Let me take you back, back, back...all the way to the 1990s.

Before that, there were certainly things you wanted to have as an American teen…a Members Only jacket, maybe. Or a Benetton sweater. Certain brands were recognizable. But by and large, you wanted your stuff to fit in: puffy socks, Velcro sneakers, or a drop-waist dress. The brand didn't matter so much. One lace hair bow was as good as another. If anything, street fashion meant that there was a certain cache in not having exactly what everyone else had.

Then…Tom Ford went to Gucci, and overnight, Main Street's obsession with high-end fashion logos exploded. After college, all the young women I was waitressing with were saving their money to buy Chanel sunglasses. Brands like Coach, that previously had relied on the shape of their bucket bag to be recognizable, came out with patterns with their logo plastered all over them. Then it was Timberland. Then Calvin Klein. Everyone became a walking billboard, and there were major consequences for how we viewed stuff and its role in our lives. First, it heightened the whole idea of status symbols. Suddenly, everyone had to be carrying a high-end purse with a collectible watch and couture sunglasses. Throw in a logo T-shirt for good measure. What it did to our sense of self is heighten the importance of what we visibly carry into any situation. Our goods became far more important than the invisible things, like our expertise or winning personalities.

It also extended into adulthood, the teenage preoccupation with "safety" manifested as having the right thing. Women in their twenties became mini Wonder Women, but instead of protecting themselves with wrists cuffs, they felt inured to the injustices of first jobs and bad dates with Bulgari B.zero1 rings on their fingers and Prada triangles on their shoes—items they would never have considered spending their entire paychecks on just a year before.

Of course, the snake rapidly began to eat its own tail. Pressure to wear status permeated every socioeconomic class, which led to the democratization of these symbols. If one class aspired to own a Birkin bag, another was busing tables to buy a LeSac that said LeSac all over it.

Outlet malls started cropping up as high-end brands discovered there was a secondary market for unsold goods. (Not to burst your bubble, but as I mentioned in Chapter One, almost everything in these malls is made at a lower quality tier.) Bargain hunting for these brands became a blood sport. eBay exploded into an online bazaar for women looking to unload last year's, last season's, last week's haul. But if one woman is wearing a Fendi Baguette bag she bought for $2,000 and her friend has one she found on eBay for $200, what is the bag really worth? And what does wearing it really convey?

Then, almost immediately, there was an explosion

of fakes. Fake bags, fake shoes, counterfeit watches, carbon-copy wallets. It was almost like performance art, stripping away any illusion that we covet these high-priced things because they are more beautiful, better made, or longer lasting. No. We wanted these objects to telegraph one thing only: I can afford this. I am successful. I have money. Respect me.

In Los Angeles, where I am based, we joke that people arrive and immediately rent a house they can't afford, lease a car they could never buy, and put new boobs on their credit card. It's a world of projection. *If I look like I have the life I want, the life will follow.*

Here is the painful truth, though: most of the time, it doesn't. What does follow is a crushing amount of debt and a ridiculous amount of clutter. I can't help my clients with the debt, but I am called in to help them figure out why they have closets full of stuff that was bought to convey that they have an enviable life.

> **If I look like I have the life I**
> **want, the life will follow.**
> **Here is the painful truth, though:**
> **most of the time, it doesn't.**

The inherent problem with this Clutter Magnet is that it is never satisfied. If you think you need stuff to command respect, the hole you are trying to fill is bottomless.

Cultivating Solid Self-Respect

I probably don't need to tell you that if you are trying to magnetize Self-Respect with clutter or relying on a handbag to convey to the world that you belong, there are some serious underpinnings to your Self-Respect that we need to scrutinize.

Even the person who has it all, Jeff Bezos, wasn't satisfied with his life on earth. He had to build a rocket to spend less than eleven minutes in space. Imagine the Self-Respect he would have felt if he had taken the monetary value of his rocket and spent it on public education. Or ending hunger in the United States. Or eliminating fossil fuels. Try to make a difference in the world, and you'll get Self-Respect by the bucketful.

I work with a screenwriter named Tanya who moved here from New York and had to go on a lot of pitch meetings. Initially, Tanya would drive her writing partner crazy trying to pick out an outfit for each meeting. Her partner, meanwhile, would just reach into her closet that morning for whatever was clean and pressed. As each meeting felt like it had very high stakes, their different approaches were causing a lot of tension between them.

Finally, in the waiting room at Sony one morning, the partner pointed out that everyone else waiting was dressed casually, and that by trying so hard, my client was under-cutting her status. "They want us to be the smartest people in the room, not the fanciest. Confidence is understated."

As Tanya looked around at everyone else's jeans and crisp T-shirts, she had a huge aha moment. Dressing like she was heading to a luncheon instead of like she was ready to roll up her sleeves and get to work was hurting her.

She called me in a few days later to help her make over her closet to match the needs of her life rather than the idea of her life. "Tracy," she said, "in my teens, clothing was armor, right? It could make you feel safe. Safe from the mean girls. And then in my twenties, it was about having the 'right' thing. And somewhere along the line I missed that I grew up. I don't need those tokens to tell me who I am. If anything, it's embarrassing. I'm embarrassed that I am trying to get a room full of strangers to respect my outfit and not my talent."

Don't be mistaken, I love certain brands—ones that are synonymous with good taste and quality products that last a lifetime. I don't mind if a client recognizes my tote and says, "Oh Clare V.! I love her Midi Sacs, and I have one of her cross-body bags."

I am not saying that you need to scrub all recognizable clothing and accessories from your life. What I am saying is that if you are relying on a triangle or a set of interlocking letters to tell the world that you're worth its time, then we need to examine that.

In my experience, my clients who rely on logos got stuck for three reasons: they don't trust their own taste, they don't trust that they have enough stature, or they are truly afraid that they are being judged and their accessories make them feel safe.

If you are choosing between two bags, will you always go for the one with the logo on it? If so, ask yourself why. Imagine yourself going into a high-pressure situation in unrecognizable clothes, a job interview, or a reunion. How do you feel? What does that bring up for you?

Can I invite you to run an experiment? I don't want you to replace your wardrobe, but the next time you buy something, can it be unplaceable? Logo free?

Can you trust that whatever you want is good enough or nice enough just because you want it?

One day, I was on-site with a client's interior designer, Mary, who spends her days moving from meetings and presentations with her own celebrity clients to construction sites. Hard hat on, hard hat off. This morning, as we were waiting for the architect, I admired Mary's gray cargo pants, which she had paired with some simple flats and a Breton T-shirt.

"Kirkland from Costco!" she proudly exclaimed loudly enough for anyone on the site to overhear, including our fancy client, who was looking at tile samples. "Look!" She dropped into a deep squat. "They stay put no matter what I need to inspect. Aren't they fabulous?! I went back and got them in a few colors."

To me, that is the epitome of trusting your own taste and your own eye. Mary understood the demands of her high-profile job and her own brand. She wears a big Rolex and always has a manicure. But she is confident enough in herself to tell an Oscar-winning client, "Oh, you have to go to Costco and get these pants!"

When it comes to the question of stature, I find that my women clients can easily lose track of what they bring into the room, especially if they are Gen X or older. Having been raised in a society that tells women that appearance is their primary contribution, it can be hard for them to remember that their expertise is their value.

Nowhere is this more ironic or painful than with my clients who are actual experts. They can be some of my worst logo offenders because competing with men for the same opportunities at the outset of their careers was hard. They think they have to have the Cartier LOVE bracelet sticking out from the sleeves of their lab coat, or Chanel shoes below their judicial robe. Their closets are bursting with these false talismans that somehow their graduate degrees didn't confer.

I ask these women if they can imagine shifting their status token from superficial accessories to symbols of their jobs, like their stethoscopes. As with Nina, my lawyer, I ask, "Could the fact that you do this job be enough to make you feel entitled to do this job? Can you simply *embody* everything you have accomplished in your career?"

Last, I have women who rely on these items to feel, in a word, safe. Growing up, did you have a peer group that demanded everyone dress exactly alike? You're not alone. It's how we communicate *I belong to this tribe, I belong to these people*. But when do you individuate? And if your friends are so catty or judgmental that you only feel inured to it if you are wielding your handbag like a shield, you might need new friends.

> **Could the fact that you have this job be enough to make you feel entitled to do this job?**

Also, this could be something you have fallen prey to later in life. Many of my mom clients felt like they had a good sense of self until their kids started school. Then, suddenly, they felt like there was a new peer group judging them and a uniform they needed to wear to fit in at pickup.

We are hardwired to assess the dynamics and values of social groups and adjust. But ask yourself, do I truly like this Lululemon jacket, or do I just want it because all the other moms in the schoolyard are wearing it? Then remind yourself that you are not fourteen anymore. If the jacket is practical and helpful—with maybe a zippered pouch for a cheese stick—then great. But if you are tempted to buy it even though it only comes in colors that make you look washed-out, then you are buying it for the wrong reason.

Ask yourself the question again: *why* are you buying it? You will not respect yourself more because you have more stuff. In fact, it can easily result in the exact opposite.

I've skied since I was young and belong to a skiing family. When we meet up at my brother's house in Utah every winter, I get to do one of my favorite things *and* I get to see all my favorite people and make the most cherished memories.

The slopes are definitely an arena where even the most label-averse people become logo addicts as they try to project their level of expertise with their gear. *Oh, you have a Moncler jacket? Those are your Rossignol skis? You must be a serious skier.* But anyone can stand around in a $1,000 jacket.

I decided years ago that instead of buying the latest logo-laden ski clothes every season, I would invest in a couple of quality pieces, take good care of them, and have them for a very long time. So long, in fact, that I still wear a White Stag ski sweater that I got during my senior year of high school. Over time, it has moved from outdated to retro to vintage to back in fashion.

Of course, all the money I've saved on new ski apparel over the years is money I can spend on flying to visit my family and ski with them, to make those invaluable memories. Not wearing shiny, new clothes doesn't detract from that. In fact, being high-fived on the slopes by a young hotshot for how cute my vintage sweater is always makes my day.

Summing It Up

Ultimately, true Self-Respect is opting out of a system that asks us to give away chunks of our net worth to the fashion industry instead of investing that money in travel, experiences, or education to propel our lives forward. Or in a nice 401(k) that will give us long-term security. The Self-Respect that is powerfully magnetic is the kind that doesn't need to be conspicuous.

When I was a senior in college, sitting in my last econ class, the professor wrote $10,000 on the chalkboard (yes, I was in college during the chalkboard days). Then he made two columns. In one column, he showed us what we could have in ten years if we put that money in a low-interest savings account. In the other, he showed us what would happen if we quickly racked up that much in credit card debt we couldn't pay off.

	Savings Account	Credit Card Debt
10 years	$36,000	If you only make the minimum payment on $10,000 worth of credit card debt, it will take 344 months to pay it off.
		In that time, you will pay an additional $15,239.61 in interest.

So that ten grand could either earn us $26,000 or cost us $15,000. He then proceeded to tell us that, as graduating seniors, our mailboxes were about to fill up with credit card offers. Lots of them. And while $10,000 was a great sum of money, it was very easy to fall into that much debt without breaking a sweat. He was imploring us to not go into credit card debt. I scoffed at the mere suggestion. *Me?*

I had been lucky enough to go to a public university and graduate without school loans. I was spending the summer waitressing at the busiest restaurant in town. All with plans to save money for my move to the big city of Los Angeles.

I was saving money and ignoring the credit card offers. I had it made.

Then, a friend called and suggested we take a trip. I didn't have enough to pay for the trip, but it just so happened that a credit card with a zero-percent introductory APR has shown up that day. Seemed easy enough. Get the cash, take the trip, and then pay it off.

I took the trip but didn't pay down the balance as quickly as I'd thought I would. I moved to LA sooner than anticipated and found a job, but I was making so much less money than at my waitressing job. And my new apartment needed furniture. Easy—put it on the card.

I don't have to tell you the rest, but in what felt like the blink of an eye, I had $10,000 in credit card debt and was only making the minimum payments. Every month when I made the payment, I thought about what my professor had said, and it chipped away at my Self-Respect.

I had always worked and proudly supported myself. My grandmother had taught me about compound interest, yet there I was, so stressed about money all the time. One day, I took my last dollar that I had until payday and bought a lottery ticket. I won ten dollars and my first thought was, "Yay, I have enough to eat Taco Bell for the next ten meals." This was back when a burrito was a dollar. But as the thought settled in, I knew I couldn't live like that anymore.

I had to change. I had to. I read all I could about debt reduction. I got a second job. I created a budget. I put everything I had into paying down my credit card debt. With focus, drive, and confidence.

You know what happened the day I reached a zero balance? I had a spring in my step and a Self-Respect I'd never felt before. I had gotten myself into a bad situation, but I got myself out of it through hard work. I had tried to buy confidence by spending money I didn't have on things I didn't need. In the end, the confidence and Self-Respect came from what I had known all along: hard work. When I think back to what that professor said to us, I am reminded of this quote from *The Wizard of Oz*:

The Scarecrow: Then why didn't you tell her before?
Glinda: Because she wouldn't have believed me. She had to learn it for herself.

I had to learn Self-Respect for myself. And you can too.

How do we attain Self-Respect? By giving back. By sharing our talents to make the world a better place. By helping someone who needs a hand. Can you volunteer at an after-school reading program? Walk a housebound neighbor's dog? And remember, nothing will make you respect yourself more than being of service.

7

magnetize your real purpose

"The purpose of life is to be happy... Many think that happiness is to be found outside us in material things, but actually it's something that comes from within, from warm heartedness and concern for others."

DALAI LAMA

WHEN I FIRST MET JANINE, SHE HAD HER HANDS full as a single mother caring for her child with special needs. She had called me in to help her set up her home to function efficiently for them. What I found were cartons and *cartons*...of art supplies. They were taking up the entire second bedroom, making the ground floor cramped and challenging terrain for her son to navigate in his wheelchair. When I asked her about the obstacle course, she explained, "I'm an art teacher. And supplies are expensive, so when there's a sale, I leap on it."

"Could your school store them?" I asked.

"Oh," she said, her shoulders falling. "Well…I don't actually have a job right now."

It turned out that she had left teaching when the extent of son's medical needs became apparent. Each year, she planned to return, and each year, he required another intervention.

"So," I asked, "how do you feel when you buy these paints and tools?"

"I feel like a teacher," she confessed. "I feel a sense of purpose."

I see this so frequently. Typically, clients who have amassed in excess professional accessories, work clothes, or books in their area of interest are all craving to be able to get out there in the world and do something that they feel matters.

An obstacle—internal or external—holds them back, however, from putting themselves out into the world. As an alternative, they do the safer, easier, more *comfortable* thing, which is to buy the related accessories.

What they *want* is to attract the pursuit that will make them feel like they're using their time well and investing in something rewarding. Instead, they attract stuff. The stuff then becomes a wonderful distraction from their missing sense of purpose. The stuff must be acquired, returned, organized, reorganized, cleaned, repaired, and managed. But unless your purpose is literally amassing a rare and priceless collection of something, this is just busywork. And the stuff is just clutter.

In this chapter we'll look at how to take your innate magnetism and redirect it from attracting that clutter to attracting your purpose.

What Stands in the Way

In my clients, I see two main emotions that keep them from exploring their purpose and keep them magnetizing clutter: fear of failure and fear of commitment. Just in case you thought there were some people who are magically born with high levels of confidence that they can start a business, a grad program, or a project with absolutely no fear that the end result will be moving back in with their parents, I have to start by telling you that we are all afraid to fail.

As Napoleon Hill famously wrote, "No man ever achieved worthwhile success who did not, at one time or other, find himself with at least one foot hanging well over the brink of failure."

I would argue that if the idea of a pursuit doesn't scare you a little bit, it's actually not worth doing. If you are 100 percent confident you can pull something off without any risk, it's probably not the area of your life where you will continue to grow, change, and be excited every day. For example, starting my business was easy. People needed help, and I loved providing it. But *growing* my business took real bravery. Hiring and training employees; allowing them to represent me, my brand, and my methodology; and figuring out all our internal policies was scary. What if I made a mistake and somehow wiped out everything I had built as a one-woman operation? But operating on my own was no longer sustainable. I had to jump into it, and it was terrifying.

I am not going to tell you to stop being afraid. Because, first of all, no one in history has ever stopped feeling a feeling because someone else told them to. (If that worked, we'd all only see a therapist once.) Second, because as Joey from *Friends* said to Rachel when she stopped pursuing a job in fashion to stay at her dead-end job at Central Perk, "You need the fear!" The fear is actually productive. It can propel us, as long as we don't let it drive the bus.

James Hayton and Gabriella Cacciotti, professors of entrepreneurship at Warwick Business School, identified seven sources of fear for entrepreneurs in their research:[1]

* Opportunity costs
* Financial security
* Ability to fund the venture
* Personal ability/self-esteem
* Potential of the idea
* Threats to social esteem
* The venture's ability to execute

Interestingly, in this scholarship, these fears didn't all have a negative impact. It turned out that worries concerning opportunity costs, personal financial security, or ability to obtain funding were all positively associated with persistence. These specific fears turned out to be *motivational*. I can attest to that. I was willing to do whatever it took to create financial security for myself and my employees—the fear of going out of business motivated me to try harder.

In contrast, Hayden and Cacciotti found that when entrepreneurs worry about the potential of their idea or their ability to execute it, those fears tend to be paralyzing. It can lead to endless number crunching becoming the primary driver and avoidance mechanism for making a mistake. Or, in my clients' cases, they amass clutter—specifically stuff they think they need to start a business—rather than take action on their ideas.

Back when I was a personal assistant to a highly sought-after TV director, I had a friend, Amy, who got a job working for a woman who had produced several success-ful films before marrying and having children. This woman wanted to get back into producing, but as she explained to Amy when they met, she *desperately* needed an assistant. Someone who could read all the scripts sent to her home, help her short-list the good ones, and get those projects rolling.

Amy leaped at the chance.

When she arrived at the job, she found a lovely space above the woman's garage, but it was piled with office supplies the producer had been ordering instead of reading scripts.

Once Amy finished getting the office organized, she read the piles and piles of scripts and wrote coverage on each one (a short summary of the story and rating of the quality). Then, she went back to her boss's home office in the main house to present her top three choices and encour-age her boss to set up meetings with the writers.

Instead, her boss had decided that if she was going to start hosting meetings, it would be best to do them in

Amy's office in case the children were home, and so Amy's little office needed to be redecorated. Suddenly Amy was running all over town with fabric swatches and bookcase stain samples. Once *that* was finally completed, instead of reaching out to writers and scheduling those meetings, she began assigning Amy her personal tasks—buying and returning all the trappings of a career—even down to what she thought would be the "right" postage stamps for her brand. Amy realized that what had seemed like a port of entry into her dream career was becoming a dead-end.

Finally, when Amy had had enough, she sat her boss down and said, "You were a really great producer. But you don't actually seem to want to do that anymore. Which is *fine*. But be honest with yourself. If you're not doing this out of fear of failure, well, get over that. But if you're not doing it because it doesn't fulfill you anymore, then *find something else*." And she quit.

In confronting her boss, Amy hit on the two challenges that turn my clients struggling with Real Purpose into Clutter Mavens: fear of failure and not knowing how to figure out where to channel their energies.

I had another client whose daughter had just graduated from college with a great idea for a new weight-loss energy drink that also balanced your chakras. She took that first post-graduation credit card I just warned you about

and bought every piece of commercial kitchen equipment known to humankind. She rented a table at the local
farmer's market and was off to the races. She was full speed
ahead, seemingly fearless.

Months later, her parents called me to help move her
out of her apartment when she could no longer afford it.
Turns out that she was fearful after all. Her fear kept her
from doing any research into health code regulations and
learning that you can't cook up any old brew in your kitchen
without a license. But once she had to start paying rent for
a commercial space, she had to raise the cost of the drinks,
and her sales went down. Things rapidly spiraled. One of
the best ways to pretend you don't have a fear of failure is to
not slow down enough to gather all the information. When
we were packing her up to move back home, she was not
only processing her newly acquired debt but her lack of
planning. They were some hard-earned lessons, but they set
her up for success in the future.

If that feels like you, perhaps look at that list above and
decide if you could shift some of your fear into one of the
motivational categories and off the paralyzing categories.
Because fear itself isn't bad as long as we don't take it as an
automatic cue to back down, lower ambitions, and play it
safe. As Gavin de Becker, author of *The Gift of Fear*, says,
"True fears and unwarranted fears may at times feel the

same, but you can tell them apart. True fear...will be based upon something you perceive in your environment or your circumstance. Unwarranted fear or worry will always be based upon something in your imagination or your memory. Worry is the fear we manufacture; it is a choice."

When my clients give into unwarranted fear and the hunger to do something is still running, that's when they start overbuying to make themselves feel productive. It never works.

The Value of Trying Things On

The other major source of paralysis-induced overbuying that I see in my clients is the fear of commitment. They are as scared of success as failure. *What if I try something and it goes well, and then I'm stuck doing it? I love baked goods, but what if I actually hate running a bakery?*

Then you will shut it down or find a way to make a graceful exit.

You are not voluntarily signing yourself up for prison. This isn't a mandatory life sentence. This is a dress you are trying on. You can only make so many good guesses about a dress from the sidewalk. You really need to get in there and put it on your body. Walk around in it. Sit down in it. It's the same for your Real Purpose.

Amy's boss could have read some scripts, met with some writers, optioned a project or two, and *still* not have been committed, but she would at least have given herself the opportunity to see how it felt. Either Amy's boss might have found that, once she was back in the saddle as a movie producer, all her fears would have fallen away and she would be off to make a new film. Or she would have found that this profession was no longer the best fit and she needed to evolve.

Either way, she would have really clear actionable data. Good or bad. Yes or no.

Instead, she kept herself stuck and distracted with this Clutter Magnet. With trying to fill the lack of purpose in her life with endless trips to Staples and Office Depot.

As I've mentioned, before I started dClutterfly, I was pursuing an acting career in Los Angeles. And it felt like a Sisyphean task. I was good but not great. I had some connections but not enough. And the constant rejection was impossible to contend with. I knew I had something to say and thought acting was the only avenue. Through it all, I convinced myself that I was only the perfect audition outfit away from booking a big job. I was forever looking for the business suit that screamed "young CEO." Or the cozy sweater that implied "got-it-all-together Mommy." Or the jean jacket that yelled out "punk—but not too punk." These outfits (which actively contributed to my aforementioned credit card debt) were going to make my career. But I'm sure you can guess the ending of this story... They didn't. They didn't make a speck of difference. In fact, as one casting director said to me when I came in to read for an 1800s period piece in my nightgown, "You know, we have an excellent costume department here, so they can imagine you in proper attire."

Meanwhile, as I was trudging along and trying to break into acting, I was *loving* my assistant job. Loving it. It was new and interesting every day, and I was solving problems on a high level. Moreover, I was making someone's life better. I shined at it. In fact, I was so good that the director I worked for started recommending me to his friends for what turned out to be organizing jobs on weekends or on my days off. Someone's grandparents had passed, and they needed help sorting through the paperwork. Someone else had taken down all their holiday decorations, and they were all in a heap in their guest room. So off to organizing I went. And I loved this work even more.

A couple things happened pretty quickly: I lost interest in buying audition outfits and accessories. All the stuff I thought I needed to convey that I belonged. And pretty soon, I stopped wanting to go to auditions. I didn't want to fly out of work in the middle of the day to go pretend to enjoy eating frozen pizza.

When my boss left town for a month, I put word out that I was available, and my little flip phone started ringing like crazy. At some point, a friend said, "You know you have a business here?" It had never occurred to me that it was a business, only that I loved doing it. I hung out a shingle, and dClutterfly was born. I had finally found my purpose and dressing the part was easy. Button-down shirt, jeans, and comfy sneakers. My uniform fit my passion, and I was liberated from trying to buy the perfect outfit for a job I was never going to get. I was able to focus on a job and clients that I loved.

How to Find Your Purpose

If, however, your challenge isn't fear of failure or commitment but rather having no idea where to channel your enthusiasm, there are some wonderful tools in the business world that can help you find your Real Purpose.

In Japanese culture, it is a common belief that we all have an *ikigai*, meaning "a reason for being" or "a path to fulfillment." What I love about this model, and what modern productivity and motivation researchers also love about it, is that it looks at fulfillment along four metrics. Your path to fulfillment has *four* ingredients, not just one. What you love, what you're good at, what the world needs, and what you'll get paid for.

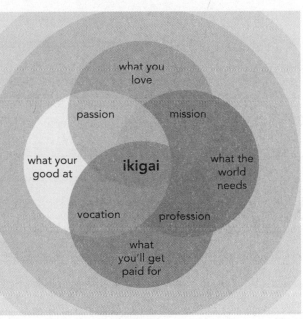

Here is the key that could have helped Amy's boss, the woman who was trying to create the perfect office environment instead of working in the office: not all four components need to get filled equally at all stages of life! Maybe in your twenties you don't mind earning less to work for a nonprofit. You love the work, and the world needs you to do the work—but you may not be good at it yet, and you're not very well paid. Your *ikigai* is still in balance because you're getting each of the components fulfilled to the extent needed for that stage in your life.

Then you get into your thirties, and maybe you leave the nonprofit for a job where you take what you are now good at and still love, and you leverage it into a better paying job in the private sector. The earning component takes the lead because you're looking ahead to raising a family and perhaps starting your own organization in your fifties.

If, however, you currently really want to be letting what you love and what the world needs be your driving force, you won't feel fulfilled in an I-hate-it-but-the-money-is-great job. Knowing which stage you're in and what you want to lean into will help you see if you're fulfilling your Real Purpose.

Amy's boss was good at making movies and had certainly been paid well in the past to do it. But perhaps she didn't love it anymore and didn't think it would make the world any better. What she needed to do, instead of buying color-coordinated file folders in bulk, is start the hard work of asking herself, "What's next?"

Margaret Gould Stewart, the vice president of product design and responsible innovation at Facebook for many years, puts it slightly differently. She says we need to be looking for the role where we feel useful, inspired, respected, and like we're growing.[2] But she also emphasizes that we do not need to fulfill all four needs equally in every role. In fact, trying to be fulfilled equally in every aspect of our lives can have the opposite effect. We end up not showing up fully anywhere—at home, at work, or at play—so we feel like we are failing everywhere instead of finding fulfillment.

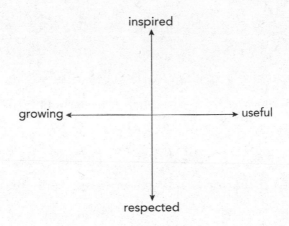

This is certainly applicable in our gig economy. I know so many people who do one job that makes them feel useful and respected (and secure and remunerated). And then they have another role that inspires them and pushes them to grow as they try to turn their passion into a business.

If you dream of becoming a jewelry maker, maybe the answer for you isn't simply leaving your secure job as a book-keeper to make jewelry, which can feel like a paralyzing all-or-nothing decision. But maybe it's deciding to see if you can shift your hours to four days a week, and devote Fridays to making jewelry and Saturdays to selling it at local artisan markets or online. Then, instead of creating a scary ultimatum for yourself that feels like doing a high dive into a thimble, the journey becomes a series of manageable decision points.

If the pursuit starts to fill the passion quadrant as well as the profession quadrant, then you might start to expand that effort and inch away from the other work. Gradually. Or not.

We are living in an era where, between Etsy and social media, we are expected to monetize every hobby, and everyone has to have a side hustle. It's no longer enough to make art; you have to sell it. It's no longer enough to cook; you have to shoot well-lit videos of you doing it and get followers. We are losing the ability to make things for the joy of making them. If a grandpa makes a soufflé and doesn't post about it—is it still delicious? I cannot emphasize this enough: your purpose may not make money or get a zillion likes, and it can still be the thing that makes you the happiest.

> **Your purpose may not make you any money.**

Is it enough to knit sweaters for friends and family or sell them to benefit a local charity near and dear to your heart? Jen Ellis, the woman who made Senator Bernie Sander's inauguration mittens out of recycled sweaters, has always donated 100 percent of her profits to Meals on Wheels in Vermont. And when she gave the senator those mittens, she never intended them to become famous. She just made them out of the goodness of her heart and to keep his hands warm.

Simply volunteering can be hugely beneficial if you can't make a big life pivot and want to increase your sense of purpose. In the *Wisconsin Longitudinal Study on the Health Benefits of Volunteering*, researchers found consistent improvements in mental and physical well-being just from small commitments to helping others.[3] There are endless organizations that need hands. Nothing gives us more sense of Real Purpose than being of service or sharing our knowledge, kindness, and time to make someone else's life better. Magnetize this feeling instead of a closet full of office supplies.

Your Purpose Is Messy

I also have some news for you if you've been looking for your purpose on social media: Real Purposes aren't pretty. I literally make things pretty for a living, and *my* Real Purpose isn't pretty.

It's messy.

I leave a client's house at the end of the day exhausted emotionally and physically, covered in dust and grime, and sore from heaving boxes. But I feel deeply fulfilled.

As someone who works in Hollywood, take it from me. While being on the cover of magazines looks beautiful and pristine, even models (and actors) are holding uncomfortable positions in uncomfortable clothes for hours and hours under hot lights. Before the beautiful cake came the flour-coated kitchen, the melted chocolate spill, and the sprinkle explosion. But because of social media, we have become addicted to the pretty end product. We want the work to look like a movie montage, and the end result to be glamorous.

Fifteen years ago, I started a nonprofit organization called OneKid OneWorld with a childhood friend named Josh. We provide an educational foundation for children in primary up through secondary school in impoverished communities throughout Kenya and Central America, which gives them the opportunity for a better and brighter future. We go into schools in remote areas that are barely operating, and we bring them what they need. We provide books, desks, and classrooms, and we pay teachers' salaries—whatever is required to keep their doors open and the education on track for these children.

> **Because of social media,**
> **we have become addicted to**
> **the pretty end product.**

We started this because, in 2006, Josh went to Darfur to help raise funds to build a medical clinic in a refugee camp. Over two weeks, he was struck by how the camp was mostly filled with women and children and how desperately they were trying to create a normal life. Classrooms had been set up outside for the kids. Women who could teach were teaching in these makeshift classrooms. Every afternoon, groups of kids had a soccer game going. All he had been able to bring in were a few soccer balls, boxes of pens, and some paper. To the kids there, he had brought gold. It occurred to him how little stuff was needed to start a school.

While he was there, he met a Kenyan doctor and nurse who told him about an all-girls school in Kenya that needed a science lab built so the students could study science, take their national science exams, and graduate. The cost of the lab was $25,000. When he got back to Los Angeles, he called me up and asked me to help him raise the money.

I was in an in-between place in my life. My organizing company, dClutterfly, was taking off, and I was loving what I was doing. But I was single, had no kids, and was taking advantage of all the fun LA had to offer in the early 2000s. But something was missing, and I had no idea what it was. I agreed to throw the fundraiser, and we had the money in under two hours. It was an amazing sense of accomplishment. To do something for someone else just because I could. For no reason other than to help them.

Six months later, after the science lab was built, Josh

and I decided to take a few volunteers to visit the school in Kenya. When I say that trip changed my life, it is the understatement of the century.

I will never forget driving uphill on the dusty road, falling in love with the beauty of Kenya in a rattle trap of a Land Rover, and turning the corner to see one hundred girls lined up and waiting for us. It is the closest I will ever come to knowing what birthing a child must feel like. Then, over the next few days, we got to spend time with the girls and hear their stories as they tried to convey the grand significance this science lab and eventual graduation would have on their life trajectories. In addition to being indescribably uplifting, it was also incredibly humbling. To realize I could do something that was fairly easy to me—throw parties—and build something that would change someone else's life for no compensation and just to be of service gave me a sense of Real Purpose I had never felt.

When I got back to LA, investing time, energy, and love into building on what we had started in Kenya got me out of bed in the morning. I worked on it every weekend and late into the night. We started traveling a couple times a year to Kenya and Central America to watch school after school be rebuilt.

Around the time we were starting the organization, we

were approached by a woman who wanted to partner with us. She was starting a nonprofit doing complementary work. We had a couple meetings, but each time, her focus seemed to be on set designing a nonprofit rather than just doing the work. She wanted to talk about whether LA or New York was better to have an office. How many staff members we were going to hire. The meeting was all about logistics on the home front with no planning on how to accomplish the changes she wanted to make. We passed on partnering with her. We later learned that she had spent her initial round of funding on a beautiful space, a full staff, iMacs for everyone, and a satellite location in New York. Within a year, she had run out of money and closed her doors without having helped a single orphanage. She was too deep in her Clutter Magnet of trying to curate the trappings instead of focusing on doing this important work. Meanwhile, fifteen years and twice as many schools later, I still believe in our mission and am still doing my full-time, non-paid job with Josh. We run a thriving organization from our kitchen tables on old laptops. It may not be pretty, but we get the job done.

If you have a lack of Real Purpose, try being of service. Just four hours a week. Or one weekend a month. Give yourself and your knowledge to help others, and you will see how quickly you feel that pride. And remember, doing the thing you love that is your highest and best calling is probably going to involve a little slog. But that is exactly what will make you feel proud of yourself at the end of the day!

It's so important in our Instagrammed world not to just look like you're doing the thing or have the stuff of someone who's doing the thing, but actually becoming that person. I can buy running gear, but it doesn't make me someone who runs. That woman could outfit an entire office to look like a nonprofit, but that doesn't mean anyone benefited from her short-lived operation.

The internal identity shift that comes with pursuing our Real Purpose isn't going to happen while shopping.

Similarly, if something is hard, that doesn't mean that you're doing it badly. It just means that you're doing it. You may start your new business in a good season when there is high demand for your offering and make a good profit. Then you may have a quiet period. This is normal. We are a culture addicted to growth, but business success is cyclical. You hope over time that those cycles are moving gradually upward, so the bottom of the next wave is just the height of an old upswing. But finding and building and maintaining your Real Purpose will require stick-to-it-iveness.

This is where multi-level marketing businesses, or MLMs, attract people—because the part at the beginning where you commit to buying hundreds of dollars' worth of face cream, leggings, or vitamin supplements is easy. The part where you have to sell it is much harder. So many people get sucked in by the high of starting a business that they forget that the back end isn't going to come with that kind of boost.

I have helped more than enough clients empty their garages of boxes and boxes of heartbreaking crap that they failed to sell. I can say with certainty that it's important to think through the tough part—the slog phase—and prepare for that as thoroughly as getting excited about potential success.

I also have a lot of clients who are the lead parent in their household and used to have a very high-octane job. Being a parent can be very fulfilling, but it is not by anyone's account a high-octane role. Potty training doesn't come close to the thrill of closing the deal. Or making partner. Or winning salesperson of the year.

So, they overprepare for the role. They buy the bottle warmer, the bottle brush, the bottle rack, and the special bottle sanitizer that negates the need for the brush or the rack. They buy more educational videos than there are hours in their child's life. They buy ten of one item that will be outgrown momentarily. And the toys. So. Many. Toys.

Somehow this makes them feel that parenting is comparable to running a multinational corporation—look at all this stuff they have to keep track of! These are typically the parents who will confide that they are not enjoying parenting much.

Here is a little thought to mull over if you are grappling with parenting and Real Purpose: your child may not check both boxes for you. For some parents, the kid does. That's great. They're getting a twofer. For other parents, they can love their child with their whole heart and make all the essential sacrifices of sleep, sanity, and personal hygiene—and yet, they still do not feel like parenting is their highest calling.

That is OK. As Sheryl Sandberg pointed out in *Lean In*, working parents today are spending the same number of hours per week on primary childcare as stay-at-home parents did in 1975.[4] Meaning that, on top of the career you love, you are *still* giving your child a ton of attention—as much as you might have received from your own parents thirty or forty years ago.

Give yourself permission to separate the two. Maybe you go back to work sooner than you had planned or start something from home that you can do part-time.

No amount of running through buybuyBABY or Pottery Barn Kids like you're on *Supermarket Sweep* is going to make the gig fulfilling if it isn't your thing.

In conclusion, if you're feeling attracted to something—a pursuit, an endeavor—but afraid, then that is not a sign to avoid it. If you are feeling attracted to something, but it is messy, that is also not a sign to avoid it. And if exclusively tending to your home isn't making you feel fulfilled, pay attention to that.

These are all signs to give yourself a way to try on some thing new.

Summing It Up

Even with the emotional demands of caring for her son, Janene, my client who was overbuying art supplies, realized that if she didn't do something for herself, she would never be the mom she wanted to be because she would be so unhappy. And no amount of magnetizing art supplies would give her that happiness. Moreover, it wasn't fair to her son to make him the obstacle.

We cleared all the art supplies out of the house and transformed the garage into an art studio. Now she teaches after-school classes there a couple of afternoons a week. Her son enjoys participating, and she feels a sense of identity outside of her role as a mother.

The last time we spoke, I asked her if she had bought any supplies lately. She laughed and said, "Are you kidding? Even with ten kids enrolled this fall, I still have a ton to go through. But it's all getting used—*finally*."

8

magnetize lasting wisdom

"The more I read, the more I acquire, the more certain I am that I know nothing."

VOLTAIRE

IN TODAY'S WORLD, WE ALL WANT SMARTPHONES and smart appliances in our smart homes. We want doorbells that call our phones and thermostats that can wake us out of a dead sleep hundreds of miles away if a pipe bursts in our home. Everyone wants to be smarter, and that's why every week I see what I call "smart clutter." People who compulsively overbuy books. Collect magazines and articles. Create reference libraries they never reference. These are also my clients with closets full of audiobooks on cassette or CDs teaching them how to buy wine, write a memoir, or invest in real estate. At its worst, my clients have bookcases full of silverfish and garage libraries that have become mouse warrens. My recipe collectors have accordion folders filled with recipes torn from magazines, most of which they have never cooked. And when they finally go through them, they always find that they have duplicates or that they have memorized them.

Full confession: we have arrived at my personal clutter magnet. I can live very happily with a nice capsule wardrobe and can cook pretty much anything with one sharp knife and a good spatula, but I have trouble resisting the siren song of information.

I buy books I never read. I sign up for webinars I never finish. I pay for courses I don't complete—because before I can even get to the last module, I've signed up for three more.

In my case, I am hungry for knowledge on two main fronts. One is health and wellness and, to be totally honest, dieting. I have bought every diet book. *Wheat Belly*, *The South Beach Diet* and *Dr. Atkins' New Diet Revolution* (which, by the way, are all pretty much the same eating plan). I buy the knowledge that I think will provide the magical solution, but I already know full well that I should just skip the sweets and get to spin class a little more often. Instead, I beat myself up when I don't follow the complex prescriptions in these books.

The second category are online classes that have the potential to expand the skill set I bring to my work with clients, like classes on the science of happiness or on letting go. I see one of those, and I have clicked Order before I've even looked at my calendar. Because that's my challenge: I'm unrealistic about my time. Yes, in my retirement, I will someday go from seminar to seminar, but right now...it isn't going to happen. In the meantime, I have overcrowded my nightstand and my inbox with smart clutter.

What Gets in the Way

My client Jackie called me in because her husband, Robbie, didn't want to let go of his library, which she thought of primarily as their second bedroom. At seven months pregnant, she was itching to get in there and start preparing for their baby's arrival. But he wouldn't clear the shelves so she could repaint and fill them with toys and picture books.

As she became increasingly agitated (to the point that in-laws were called in), he finally caved and, in a fit of passive-aggressiveness, installed a giant plastic shed in the backyard and filled it with boxes of books.

This made no sense. A shed is a terrible place to store

paper, even in a dry climate like Los Angeles, and it was an eyesore. Not to mention that she wanted to put a little jungle gym in that space sometime down the road.

When I finally sat down with him, I asked Robbie what was important to him, so we could find a solution that made everyone happy. I learned that he had started his career editing documentary films, but after editing a documentary on food, he then started down a path editing unscripted food shows that became increasingly, in his words, "sophomoric." And with a baby on the way, he was afraid there would be pressure to take gigs that were less and less inspiring. "What's next?" he asked me. "Dog food competition shows?" In his mind, his library conveyed that he was a thinker—someone to be taken seriously.

We had gotten clear that what Robbie really needed was to make a career shift, and over the next eighteen months, the importance of the books would start to fall away. I suggested a coach who could help him map a path back to doing the kind of editing work he really wanted, while still contributing to the household budget to a satisfactory degree.

Then we went through the books, selected the ones that were genuinely meaningful to him, and found places for them in the house, integrating them into the design without clutter.

Smart clutter is one of the most symbolic categories

of clutter because rarely do we want the thing itself—
the gravy-stained cookbook or the mildewed *National
Geographic*. Robbie was probably never going to crack the
spine on any of those books again, but they represented a
part of his identity that he feared was slipping away. Which
is why it's so important to examine the things we do to reinforce that feeling of Lasting Wisdom without more stuff.

For some of my women clients, this clutter magnet is
about growing up in homes or communities that didn't
value their contributions, and they often feel like they need
to keep evidence of their beliefs in case they're challenged.
But instead of, "I'll send you the link," they say, "I have that
article around here somewhere. I'm going to find it and send
you a copy." Meaning Xerox and snail mail. By the time
it arrives, who cares anymore? And in trying to magnetize
Lasting Wisdom, they were all wasting time.

Larry, another client and retired political scientist, had one
of the sharpest minds I have ever encountered. Initially, he had
hired me because he was concerned about his collection of
filing cabinets, which lined all three walls of his garage. When
he ran out of room on those walls, he proposed to his wife that
they park their car in the driveway, so he could add a fourth
wall of cabinets. That's when she called me. Back when he
had an office, he used to keep the bulk of his files there, but
once he retired, he brought it all home—much to her chagrin.

The cabinets, each of which weighed what felt like a thousand pounds, were filled with magazine and newspaper clippings—some going back decades.

He was very resistant to the idea of eliminating any of them, but his neighborhood had flooded a couple of times, and he was open to having me help him put the filing cabinets up on blocks. (Whatever gets me in the door!)

Once we started looking through the cabinets, we found an added wrinkle. Not only were there reams and reams of yellowed newsprint, but there was also no organizational system. While Larry remembered the salient points of the articles he had filed, he could never remember what he had filed them under—By author? By topic? By name of the newspaper? It was a mess. Then he asked me if I could help him refile the thousands of clippings.

"Larry," I started, "I could absolutely charge you to do that, but I'd much rather see you spend that money on a vacation." I held up a folder of thirty-year-old articles. "So much of this thinking is outdated. Do you really need to know everyone's policy position from the eighties? Who is going to ask you about that?"

He smiled, realizing that he had allowed an essential habit from the beginning of his career to turn into a strange, comforting ritual that had taken over his garage.

"There's something about cutting the article out and

filing it, Tracy," he said. "It makes me feel like I've absorbed the information and made it mine. And in the old days, if I didn't do that, it would be incredibly hard to find the piece again. I'd have to go to the library and pull it up on the microfiche and then make a Xerox. I come from a tradition where you can't make a point without referencing the data that proves it." But Larry could see that the world had moved on. "I'm not publishing research anymore," he admitted. "I don't need all these articles."

We started by just pulling out everything from any publication that had digitized their archives, like the *New York Times*, and recycling those articles. That allowed us to remove half the cabinets right off the bat. Then we got rid of everything that was outdated or nonessential.

What Larry ended up with was one filing cabinet filled with recent pieces, which he promised to review and purge regularly. His wife, who had been dying to set up a gardening table in the garage to repot her succulents, was euphoric.

"Larry," I asked in our last session, "can you trust in this new phase of your life, that you can contribute to the conversation without needing a faded scrap of paper to back you up? Can you stop magnetizing the paper and create freedom? In your cabeza and your garage?"

He laughed and said, "Tracy, I really can."

Once Larry let go of all the files, he found that his energy shifted from information hoarding to information sharing, and he joined a politically active social group. Now he gets to talk about what he knows instead of filing it away. And he loves it when the younger members say, "Wow, Larry, you know *everything*."

Learning to Trust Our Own Wisdom

As with every single Clutter Magnet we've covered, the underlying desire here—to be a lifelong learner—is great! But if you have crossed over into accumulating clutter, then it's important to look at what is motivating you. What are you searching for? Is there an answer to a tough life problem that you feel is elusive? Is it possible that therapy might be the real key?

When it came to my addiction to classes, I had to accept that, while we always want to be growing and learning and seeking and expanding, entering my credit card number did not accomplish those things. At the end of the day, buying courses I wouldn't complete or books I wouldn't read was no better than paying for a gym membership and not going.

The next step is to look at the underlying motivation. What place are you doing it from? If you're buying these things to give yourself a gift of knowledge, great! But if you believe on some level that you are "less than," no course can solve that, not this one nor the seventh course that you won't listen to. The unread book is as much of a rebuke as the unused TheraBand or hand weights.

If this sounds familiar, what I have found helpful is to set up some really clear parameters. First, I had to declutter. That meant going through all my nonfiction books and donating the ones I would honestly never read. Ever. The ones I started five times and put down after the first chapter. Even if I get laid up in bed with a broken leg, I am not going to read those while I am convalescing. (I'll want to sink my teeth into a juicy mystery instead.)

This is what I tell clients: if you have gone on two vacations without reading that book/magazine/bonus content, it never will be. Let it go. For years, I dragged a giant, hardcover copy of *Anna Karenina* on my yearly trip to Hawaii to visit family. And guess what, I never read it. Yes, it's a great book, and it would make me a more well-read (and smarter!) person, but it's the last book I want to read on the beach.

After realizing how much space the book took up in my suitcase, I switched to a paperback version. I still didn't read that on the beach. Or when I was home from vacation. I was about to click Buy on an audio version of it when I had a conversation with myself. *Stop buying a book you clearly are not interested in reading! You have read plenty, and for whatever reason, this book doesn't speak to you. And that's OK.* It really was. No client or party host was going to give me a pop quiz on *Anna Karenina*. Not having read it didn't mean I didn't go to a good enough college, or that I don't deserve a seat at the grown-up table, or whatever else I was imbuing in it. As the very wise and fictional Stuart Smalley says, "I'm good enough, I'm smart enough, and doggone it, people like me." I felt better the second the pages hit the shelf of our local free library. It was gone within hours.

Next, I went through my computer and looked at all the unfinished courses I had downloaded. I took a deep breath, pulled out my calendar, and saw that I realistically had an hour a week to devote to taking a course. I picked two that I was the most excited to try and could truly hold myself to complete—and I deleted the rest.

Yes, I had paid a lot for them back in the day. And yes, I think I want to bake bread like Nancy Silverton. But first off, if you read my first book, you know that holding onto these courses just because I paid for them would be the seventh Emotional Clutter Block, or The Stuff I Keep Paying For. Second, there is a stand at our local farmers market that sells delicious sourdough and walking there with my partner and our dog on a Sunday morning brings me a lot of joy. Spending that time with them brings me much more happiness than kneading a pile of dough and with the same result, which is that I get to eat amazing bread.

I went through and had that same conversation with myself about every offering. Maybe I don't need a sommelier's knowledge of white wines or maybe I don't need to understand the deep science behind why eating gluten makes me feel bad.

Then I went through my computer and deleted all the articles I had bookmarked to catch up on next time I had a long flight because, truth be told, I don't enjoy reading articles on airplanes. I enjoy getting lost in a great novel or catching up on movies I haven't been able to see. But I don't want to do homework on the plane. And, after many years of traveling, I have accepted this about myself. Every time I am in the airport bookstore and pick up the newest nonfiction best seller and think, "I really should read this," I look at my noise-canceling headphones and remind myself of the great movie I will watch instead.

Meanwhile, I kept asking myself if maybe I could trust that the things I was meant to learn would come to me in other ways. For example, I love listening to educational podcasts while I drive or walk the dog. Could it be enough for me, right now, at this stage in my life—with a demanding business, a thriving charity, and a full personal life—to be able to say, "I heard Adam Grant say the most interesting thing the other day..." without running out to put the book at the top of my teetering pile?

At my last checkup, my cholesterol was a bit high, so on my doctor's recommendation, I bought a very heavy and large science book on how to lower it by cutting out sugar and white flour. Every night, I would read a couple of pages and fall asleep. I could never get to the informational part on how to really make a change. I finally gave up and considered going on medication. Then, with a quick Google search, I found the author on a podcast, listened intently on my drive to work one day, and gleaned all the information I needed. Between the notorious LA traffic and a large dog to walk, a podcast interview or an audiobook is a much better way to for me to absorb the information quickly from many prescriptive nonfiction books. And I kill two clutter magnets at one time: Free Time and Lasting Wisdom!

Moving forward, I have promised myself and my fiancé that I can't buy a new course until I have done all the assignments for the previous course. And I can't buy a new book until I've finished the ones on my nightstand. I'm not beating myself up. I'm just finding a way to place pauses before I overwhelm myself again.

Because it's not enough to remove the old smart clutter if we don't put a plan in place to prevent us from magnetizing more.

Last, if you want to magnetize Lasting Wisdom *and* eliminate clutter, nothing will help you do that like learning how to make things for yourself. Years ago, I read this super interesting cookbook called *Make the Bread, Buy the Butter* by Jennifer Reese. When she lost her job, she set out to figure out what was less expensive to buy versus make from scratch in the interest of saving money. Cleverly, she also took into account time and stress when making her final calculations. And at the end of each recipe, she tells you whether you should buy it or make it.

I love hummus, and according to her book, it's very economical and delicious to make. But somehow, I still couldn't break my Whole-Foods-hummus-in-a-plastic-tub-for-$4.98 habit. And I felt terrible every time I did it.

Cut to me meeting my fella, and I was *still* buying tubs of hummus. That's when he said, "You know, I make delicious hummus, and it's so easy. I mean, I lived in the Middle East."

"Yes, I do know it's easy to make, but no, I did not know you could make it."

Next thing I knew, he went on a quick jaunt to the same Whole Foods that had kept me in plastic tubs and bought chickpeas, tahini, and garlic. We picked a lemon off the neighbor's tree, and he whipped up the most delicious batch of hummus I had ever had. And at a fraction of the cost of Le Plastic Tub d'Hummus. A fraction! I had met my match. A guy who cared about the environment and financial security…and would keep making me the hummus I love.

He had learned the recipe when he was young and broke, traveling around the world. He carried that knowledge with him and made hummus wherever he lived. This kind of Lasting Wisdom will last us a lifetime. And I can't help but think about all the plastic he's saved.

I'm also going to make one final pitch for sewing and repairing things for yourself. If the global disruption to the supply chain has taught us anything, it's that our dependence on next-day free shipping can leave us all flat-footed when goods get stranded on cargo containers in the middle of the Pacific Ocean or at ports awaiting truckers who have left the industry. Heading into the holiday season of 2021, many shelves at my local big box stores were empty. Whole sections of our IKEA had *nothing*. And one week, I went to four drug stores to get shower gel for our guest bath, but to no avail.

I am hoping this will mark the beginning of a return to thinking of consumer goods as precious items. With inflation on the rise, we might stop and think before buying a disposable dress instead of altering one we already have. Or just sewing closed the tiny rip that the dog made in our throw pillow.

Think of all the shirts that you have taking up space in your closet and that you don't wear because they've lost a button. If you were able to sew a button back on, mend a rip, or patch a hole…those clothes could have a whole second or third life.

My friend, Nora, was sick of having to let go of jeans she

loved when she wore through the knees. However, she was living in Brooklyn, and cold knees didn't really appeal to her. Also, as a mom, she felt like her ripped jeans stage of life might have passed, so she learned the Japanese decorative stitching method of *sashiko*. Going back to the Edo period of the seventeenth century, this patterned stitching was used to reinforce fabric in vulnerable spots, or layer cloth for extra warmth. But the stitching is done in a beautiful pattern that converts a basic mend into something gorgeous and special. Plus, because she was doing it herself, she felt tremendous pride in this new skill set she was developing. Best of all, it would transform a garment she once might have considered consigned to the recycling bin into something so special that she would wear it proudly for years to come.

In short, we have to normalize a culture of fixing things and not just throwing them away. Not only is it good for the planet, but it's good for our souls.

Summing It Up

Overcoming this clutter magnet is about internalizing a new belief: that our opinions are valid, and they we don't need to *prove* ourselves in casual conversation with citations or an invitation to come see our home library—or filing cabinet cemetery.

I often feel like the wizard in *The Wizard of Oz* when I tell clients that they don't need to prove they've accrued Lasting Wisdom. It's all right between their ears—terabytes of portable storage.

CONCLUSION

you are enough

Ultimately, our goal is to know and believe that happiness is possible for us. Without the perfect outfit, organization system, or curling iron. Without the next purchase. Or the ten we've already made. We should be able to picture ourselves naked in a warm, empty space and feel serenity and peace. We can't only like ourselves with the right accessories.

Have you ever watched a toddler with a doll? The doll arrives in its package with all the accessories—the diaper, the little dress, and the changing bag and pacifier. And then, those are all stripped away in short order. Eventually, the doll is just this graying blob being dragged around by one leg. But it is *so loved*. In that child's mind, the doll is *perfect*. That is how we should feel about ourselves. We are all slightly the worse for wear. And we are perfect.

So. Here you are. You have identified your Clutter Magnet and figured out how to take active steps to get more of the feeling you want in your life—like Big Love, Self-Confidence, or Lasting Wisdom—and less stuff. Now you're in a store…or in a mood. And the siren song of something fun is calling. What can you do to breathe through it?

First, take stock. Go take a look in your closet or cupboard. I bet you already have a sweater that color—or a knife that does pretty much the same thing as that gizmo.

If that doesn't sway you, then just pause. Set a timer on your phone. I suggest twenty-four hours for every $50 you want to spend. Most likely, by the time you hear the timer go off, you will have forgotten about the turtleneck or deep conditioner.

If you still want the item, but also know that you in no way *need* it or already have turtlenecks that you never wear and tons of conditioner you have never used, then try counting your blessings. Literally. Get out a piece of paper and count them. Focusing on what you have pulls your focus off what you want.

Then, if your brain is still stuck on the pore extractor or the hairbrush that works like a blow-dryer, take stock of how much True Connection you are getting in your life. Go out of your way to have an interaction. Even a phone call.

Calling someone you know who could use a little cheering up will get you bonus points because being of service helps ground you in what is important. Volunteering for community members in need will quickly remind you that you can live a very happy life without those silver brogues.

Last, go for a run, a walk, or a game of pickleball. Hop on that at-home spin bike you already bought. Get some endorphins pumping! Remind yourself that you have the power to make yourself feel really good without shopping.

Because you do!

But in a way that is less sparkly and more sustainable. The truth is, you're not going to be happy all the time. The new purse or the flower-patterned file folder organizers are only going to get you high for a little while—and they'll always leave you wanting more. If something is genuinely making you sad, a trip to the mall may give you the short-term illusion of feeling better, but it doesn't solve anything. Especially if you come home with items that you have no room for—and can't afford.

Healthy Acquisition

We have learned a lot about what we don't want to do when it comes to acquiring from this point on. But what *is* the goal? It's what I call "healthy acquisition." Just like healthy eating, healthy acquisition allows us to do this essential activity that we also enjoy, but in a way that is holistically beneficial.

In the past, I would reward myself with food when life got stressful. I always felt really great about these treats while I was eating them—but then I'd be so mad at myself afterward. I finally had to take a hard look at that dissonance and see if I could create a new reward system. Now it's meeting up with a friend for a walk or getting a weekly pedicure with an extra leg massage. I look forward to it, feel great during it, and feel pleased with myself afterward. If there is a disconnect between how you feel while doing the activity, in this case shopping, and how you feel about it *after*, like guilt or overwhelm, then something is out of alignment. If you get home from shopping and feel a little queasy, or if it's all fun and games every month until your credit card statement arrives, then you are not acting in harmony with your highest goals for yourself.

Healthy shopping looks like this. "Wow, my makeup is all over a year old, and some of it doesn't smell so great. Let me start doing some research. OK, I found a brand I want to try with great verified reviews, renewable packaging, and no harmful chemicals. I'm so excited for it all to arrive. Oh, yay—it's here, and I love it! I look updated and fresh. Here's the bill. No sweat—it's exactly what I budgeted, and I don't even think about it."

That is a healthy acquisition cycle. You need something. You make an informed decision about what to buy. And you select something within your realistic budget. That goes for new couch pillows and spin shoes too.

Because nothing is more empowering than feeling in control of what you bring into your home and how you use your budget. When my clients make the shift to spending less on discretionary items every month, they are almost instantly calmer.

The fact is that you can take control of your spending and your home by doing the things we have covered. These steps will create a life you enjoy waking up to each day. A life in which your home is calm and easy to navigate. In which you can find the things you need easily. In which your bills are comfortable to pay. A life in which you are getting outside every day and moving your body. In which you see friends and family consistently. In which you feel useful to your community.

Those things don't come with a shopping list. Your best and most fulfilling life is not on the other side of a purchase.

I see you. And I like you exactly as you are in this moment.

Your job now is to see yourself too. Joyous. Calm. Content. Enough... And standing in an empty room.

APPENDIX

adverse childhood experience (ace) questionnaire

Finding your ACE Score
Before your eighteenth birthday:

1. Did a parent or other adult in the household **often**...
   swear at you, insult you, put you down, or humiliate you?
   or
   act in a way that made you afraid that you might be physically hurt?
   Yes   No   If yes, write "1" _____

2. Did a parent or other adult in the household **often**...
   push, grab, slap, or throw something at you?

or

ever hit you so hard that you had marks or were injured?

Yes   No   If yes, write "1" _____

3. Did an adult or person at least five years older than you **ever**...

    touch or fondle you or have you touch their body in a sexual way?

    or

    try to or have oral, anal, or vaginal intercourse with you?

    Yes   No   If yes, write "1" _____

4. Did you **often** feel that...

    no one in your family loved you or thought you were important or special?

    or

    your family didn't look out for one another, feel close to one another, or support one another?

    Yes   No   If yes, write "1" _____

5. Did you **often** feel that...

    you didn't have enough to eat, had to wear dirty clothes, and had no one to protect you?

    or

your parent(s) was/were too drunk or high to take care of you or take you to the doctor if you needed it?

Yes   No   If yes, write "1" _____

6. Were your parents **ever** separated or divorced?

Yes   No   If yes, write "1" _____

7. Was your mother or stepmother:

often pushed, grabbed, slapped, or had something thrown at her?

or

sometimes or often kicked, bitten, hit with a fist, or hit with something hard?

or

ever repeatedly hit over at least a few minutes or threatened with a gun or knife?

Yes   No   If yes, write "1" _____

8. Did you live with anyone who was a problem drinker or alcoholic, or who used street drugs?

Yes   No   If yes, write "1" _____

9. Was a household member depressed or mentally ill, or did a household member attempt suicide?

Yes   No   If yes, write "1" _____

10. Did a household member go to prison?

Yes   No   If yes, write "1"_____

Add up your "Yes" answers:

_____

This is your ACE Score.

For an explanation of your ACE Score, you can visit https://www.cdc.gov/vitalsigns/aces/pdf/vs-1105-aces-H.pdf

If you're struggling with clutter and home management to the point that it affects your daily life and relationships, please reach out to a mental health professional.

endnotes

Introduction

1. dClutterfly. Accessed March 8, 2022. https://dclutterfly .com/.

Chapter 1

1. Joseph R. Ferrari, Catherine A. Roster, and Kendall P. Crum *et al.* "Procrastinators and Clutter: An Ecological View of Living with Excessive 'Stuff.'" *Current Psychology* 37 (2018): 441–444.

2. Leonie Meier, *Synthesis Report on United Nations System-wide Initiatives related to Fashion*, United Nations Alliance for Sustainable Fashion (2021), 5.

3. Catherine A. Roster, Joseph R. Ferrari, and M. Peter Jurkat, "The Dark Side of Home: Assessing Possession 'Clutter' on Subjective Well-Being," *Journal of Environmental Psychology*, Vol. 46 (2016): 32–41.

4. Jacqueline R. Rifkin and Jonah Berger, "How Nonconsumption Can Turn Ordinary Items into Perceived Treasures," *Journal of the Association for Consumer Research*, Vol. 6 No. 3 (2021).

5. Renee Cho, "Recycling in the U.S. Is Broken. How Do We Fix It?" *State of the Planet* by Columbia Climate School, March 13, 2020.

Chapter 2

1. National Academies of Sciences, Engineering, and Medicine. *Social Isolation and Loneliness in Older Adults: Opportunities for the Health Care System* (Washington, DC: The National Academies Press, 2020).

2. Liz Mineo, "Over Nearly 80 Years, Harvard Study Has Been Showing How to Live a Healthy and Happy Life." *Harvard Gazette,* November 26, 2018. https://news.harvard.edu /gazette/story/2017/04/over-nearly-80-years-harvard-study -has-been-showing-how-to-live-a-healthy-and-happy-life/.

3. David A. Snowdon, "Healthy Aging and Dementia: Findings from the Nun Study," *Ann Intern Med* 139 (2003): 450–454.

4. Amy A. Hakim, M.S., Helen Petrovitch, M.D., Cecil

M. Burchfiel, Ph.D., G. Webster Ross, M.D., Beatriz L. Rodriguez, M.D., Ph.D., Lon R. White, M.D., Katsuhiko Yano, M.D., J. David Curb, M.D., and Robert D. Abbott, Ph.D., "Effects of Walking on Mortality among Nonsmoking Retired Men," *New England Journal of Medicine* 338 (1998): 94–99.

5. *A Dictionary of Psychology*, 3rd ed., s.v. "emotional intelligence."

6. John D. Mayer, Richard D. Roberts, and Sigal G. Barsade, "Human Abilities: Emotional Intelligence," *Annual Review of Psychology* 59 (2008): 507–536.

7. Armchair Expert. "Daniel Goleman." Armchair Expert, June 22, 2021. https://armchairexpertpod.com/pods/daniel -goleman.

Chapter 3

1. Euromonitor. Accessed March 8, 2022. https://www .euromonitor.com/.

2. Joseph M. Andreano et al. "Sex Differences in the Persistence of the Amygdala Response to Negative Material." *Social Cognitive and Affective Neuroscience*, Vol. 9 No. 9 (2014): 1388–1394.

3. Jennifer Finney Boylan, "What It Was Like to Be a Transgender Woman in 2003," *Allure*, August 24, 2015. https://www.allure .com/story/transgender-activist-jennifer-finney-boylan.

Chapter 4

1. Kiron Chatterjee, Ben Clark, Adrian Davis, and Deirdre Roher, "The Commuting and Wellbeing Study: Understanding the Impact of Commuting on People's Lives," Bristol: UWE Bristol, 2017.

2. Yoram Wurmser, "Mobile Will Account for a Third of All US Media Time This Year." *Insider Intelligence*, June 15, 2021. https://www.emarketer.com/content/nearly-third-of-all-us-media-time-will-on-mobile-this-year.

Chapter 5

1. Amit Kumar and Nicholas Epley, "Undervaluing Gratitude: Expressers Misunderstand the Consequences of Showing Appreciation," *Psychological Science*, Vol. 29 Issue 9 (2018): 1423–1435.

2. Gregory N. Bratman, J. Paul Hamilton, Kevin S. Hahn, Gretchen C. Daily, and James J. Gross, "Nature Experience Reduces Rumination and Subgenual Prefrontal Cortex Activation," *Proceedings of the National Academy of Sciences of the United States of America*, 112. June 29, 2015.

3. Oprah.com. Accessed March 7, 2022. https://www.oprah.com/own-digitaloriginals/oprahs-favorite-definition-of-forgiveness-video. March 14, 2018.

Chapter 7

1. Gabriella Cacciotti, James C. Hayton, J. Robert Mitchell, and Adres Giazitzoglu, "A Reconceptualization of Fear of Failure in Entrepreneurship," *Journal of Business Venturing*, Vol. 31 Issue 3 (2016): 302–325.

2. Margaret Gould Stewart, "The Four Dimensions of Job Fulfillment—And a Map to Find Them," Accessed March 8, 2022. Medium.com.

3. J. A. Piliavin and E. Siegl, "Health benefits of volunteering in the Wisconsin longitudinal study," *Journal of Health and Social Behavior; Washington*, Vol. 48, Issue 4 (2007): 450–64.

4. Sheryl Sandberg and Neil Scovell, *Lean In: Women, Work, and the Will to Lead* (New York: Knopf, 2013), 134.

index

A

Acts of generosity, 48
Adverse childhood experience (ACE)
    questionnaire, 199–202
Advertisements, 21–25
Alliance of Sustainable Fashion (UN), 19
Amazon, 24
Annual Review of Psychology, 56
Armchair Expert (podcast), 56

B

Bargaining, 29
Basel Action Network, 24
Beattie, Melody, 46
Becker, Gavin de, 158
Bezos, Jeff, 141
Big Love (Clutter Magnet #4), 35,
    109–132
Brown, Brené, 65
Buying. *See* Shopping
Buy Nothing groups, 60

C

Cacciotti, Gabriella, 155
Centers for Disease Control and
    Prevention (CDC), 121
Character, 133
Climate change, 19
Clothes, 13–15, 17–19, 32, 61
Clutter, 5, 11, 13–14
    history of, 15–21
    smart, 181
Clutter Blocks. *See* Emotional Clutter
    Blocks
Clutter Magnets. *See* Emotional Clutter
    Magnets
Codependency, 46–47
Codependent No More (Beattie), 46
Commuting, 91
*The Confidence Code: The Science and Art
    of Self-Assurance—What Women Should
    Know* (Kay and Shipman), 67
Consumer culture, 18

Coping strategies
  unproductive, 55, 124
COVID-19 pandemic, 10–11, 39
  and commuting, 91
  lockdown during, 1–2
Crafting, 37
Current Psychology, 14

D
Dalai Lama, 151
"Date night outfit" clutter, 10
dClutterfly, 2–3, 5, 169
Death, premature, risk of, 40
Decluttering, 58–62
Didion, Joan, 133
Donations, 31–33
Downsizing, 72

E
eBay, 32
Efficiency clutter, 91
Ellis, Jen, 166
eMarketer, 93
Emmons, Robert, 130
Emotional Clutter Blocks
  Block #1 (My Stuff Keeps Me in the
    Past), 5
  Block #2 (My Stuff Tells Me Who I
    Am), 5
  Block #3 (The Stuff I'm Avoiding), 5–6
  Block #4 (My Fantasy Stuff for My
    Fantasy Life), 6
  Block #5 (I'm Not Worth My Good
    Stuff), 6
  Block #6 (Trapped with Other People's
    Stuff), 6
  Block #7 (The Stuff I Keep Paying
    For), 6
Emotional Clutter Magnets
  Clutter Magnet #1 (True Connection),
    34, 39–63

Clutter Magnet #2 (Strong Self-
    Confidence), 34, 65–83
Clutter Magnet #3 (Free Time), 35,
    85–107
Clutter Magnet #4 (Big Love), 35,
    109–132
Clutter Magnet #5 (Self-Respect), 35,
    133–150
Clutter Magnet #6 (Real Purpose), 35,
    151–175
Clutter Magnet #7 (Lasting Wisdom),
    35, 177–192
  overview, 9–10
Emotional holes, 10
Emotional intelligence, 56
Emotional ties, 43–44
Entrepreneurs, sources of fear for, 155
Environmental justice nonprofit, 24
Environmental Protection Agency
    (EPA), 32
Everlane, 65–67

F
Fair Play (Rodsky), 96
Fallon, Jimmy, 74–75
Fears, 158–159
  sources of, 155
  unwarranted, 158–159
Feelings, 34–37
Food, 15, 25
Free Time (Clutter Magnet #3), 35,
    85–107
Friedman, Kinky, 109
Friendships, 44–45

G
Gender differences, 67–69
The Gift of Fear (Becker), 158–159
Gifts, 48
Gig economy, 165
Goleman, Daniel, 56

Goodwill, 15
Gratitude, 81, 130–131

H

Handler, Chelsea, 124
Harvard Longitudinal Study, 43–44
Hayton, James, 155
Helping, meaning of, 3–4
Hill, Napoleon, 154

I

ikigai, 162, 163
I'm Not Worth My Good Stuff
(Emotional Clutter Block #5), 6
Industrial revolution, 40–41
Isolation, 40

K

Kay, Katty, 67

L

Landfills, 19
Lasting Wisdom (Clutter Magnet #7),
35, 177–192
Lean In (Sandberg), 174
Little House on the Prairie (Wilder), 16
Lockdown, 1–2, 86
Loneliness, 44, 54

M

Make the Bread, Buy the Butter (Reese),
189
Making Space, Clutter Free (McCubbin),
5, 7
Manufacturing, 18, 19–20
Media literacy, 21–25
Meet-ups, 57
Michels, Barry, 81
Moran, Caitlin, 71
More Than a Woman (Moran), 71
Moving, 3

Multiplier, 52
Municipal solid waste, 19, 32
My Fantasy Stuff for My Fantasy Life
(Emotional Clutter Block #4), 6
My Stuff Keeps Me in the Past
(Emotional Clutter Block #1), 5
My Stuff Tells Me Who I Am
(Emotional Clutter Block #2), 5

N

National Academies of Science,
Engineering, and Medicine, 39
Need, concept of, 16
New England Journal of Medicine, 53

O

Online classes, 179
Online shopping during lockdown, 1–2
Overbuying, 159–162
Overshopping, 45–46

P

Padman, Monica, 56
Parents, moving in, 3
Possessions, 14
Premature death, risk of, 40
Pricing, 19, 20

R

Real Purpose (Clutter Magnet #6), 35,
151–175
Recidivism, 70
Recycling, 32–33
Reese, Jennifer, 189
Relationships, and health, 43–44
Retail therapy, 116
Ritual, 65–67
Rodsky, Eve, 96
Rollins, Henry, 85

S

Sandberg, Sheryl, 174
Santos, Laurie, 100, 127
Science of Happiness, 100, 127
Self-Respect (Clutter Magnet #5), 35,
  133–150
Selling, 21–25, 65–67
Sewing, 17–18
Shephard, Dax, 56
Shipman, Claire, 67
Shopping, 25–31, 50–52
  habits, breaking, 127–131
  online, 1–2
  overshopping, 45–46
Smart clutter, 177–179, 181
Smart Less (podcast), 124
Smart phones, 92–93
Snowdon, David, 44
Social connectivity, 44
Social media, 55–56
Specialness spiral, 29
Stewart, Margaret Gould, 164
Strong Self-Confidence (Clutter Magnet
  #2), 34, 65–83
The Stuff I Keep Paying For (Emotional
  Clutter Block #7), 6
The Stuff I'm Avoiding (Emotional
  Clutter Block #3), 5–6
Stutz, Phil, 81

T

Tall poppy syndrome, 67
Technology, 16
TerraCycle model, 33
Time, 85–90
  reallocation, 94
  saving, 98
Time management, 101–106
Time-saving devices, 90, 91–92
T.J.Maxx, 46
The Tools (Michels and Stutz), 81–82

Trapped with Other People's Stuff
  (Emotional Clutter Block #6), 6
True Connection (Clutter Magnet #1),
  34, 39–63
  decluttering and, 58–62
  nurturing more connection, 54–58
  overshopping to magnetize, 45–46

U

*University of Chicago Press Journal for the
  Association of Consumer Research,* 29
Unproductive coping strategies, 54, 124
Unwarranted fears, 158–159

V

Violet Grey, 65–67

W

Waldinger, Robert, 44
Walgreens, 46
Walking, 53
Weight loss, 69–76
Wellness, 69–76, 178–179
Western civilizations, 39
Wilder, Laura Ingalls, 16
*Wisconsin Longitudinal Study on the
  Health Benefits of Volunteering,* 167
Women, 67–69, 71
Worry, 159

acknowledgments

To Nicola, I am even more grateful for you this second spin around the book block. I cannot thank you enough for your tireless enthusiasm, limitless wisdom, and endless patience. Especially when it came to unwinding the clutter in my head.

To Lucinda, thank you for being the best cheerleader and best agent an author could ask for. You saw it all from the beginning. Thank you for guiding me through the tough decisions and reminding me of the importance of the message.

To Connor, navigating the moguls of publishing is a whole lot easier with your guidance and amazing spirit. Thank you for everything.

To Anna, thank you for being such a kind, thoughtful. and fantastic editor. Your notes and suggestions made this such a better book.

To the amazing team at Sourcebooks, so happy to be working with you all for a second time. Again, you hit it out of the park.

To Jessica Thelander, thank you for doing all the heavy lifting and producing such a great book.

To Jillian Rahn, you art directed such a beautiful book, especially the cover. I can't wait to see it in the bookstores and in people's homes.

To Ashley, leading my powerhouse PR team. We will shout this book from the rooftops together. Thank you for your dedication and commitment.

To my dClutterfly Team, how do I begin to thank you for helping support my life's work, helping build my company, and helping our clients every day? You are the hardest working group of folks I know. Your kindness and thoughtfulness are overwhelming. Thanks for throwing your whole heart into the weirdest/greatest job there is. You all put the "fly" in dClutterfly.

To Julie, you flipped the script on being bossy into being a boss. Proving Miss Sutherland wrong. Thanks for leading the way for 50+ years. You are my forever inspiration.

To Carrie and Liz, thank you for answering every text,

no matter inane or minuscule. Your unwavering support and friendship gets me out of bed in the morning. Or keeps me in bed, texting you both.

To Sandi, thanks for championing me every step of the way. And teaching me how to spot a really good piece on sale.

To Ian, Gannet, Ocean, Snow, and Rio, my loves, my lights, my family. There are no words for how grateful I am for all of you.

To Rich, your love, your support, and your command of the English language—really, what more could I ask for? Thank you for being the best thing that has ever happened to me. I love you. I can't wait to walk home with you.

about the author

© Rebecca Sanabria

Tracy McCubbin is the owner of dClutterfly, Los Angeles's #1 Home Organization company, as well as the author of *Making Space, Clutter-Free: The Last Book on Decluttering You'll Ever Need*. She is a regularly featured expert in major media, including the *Washington Post*, the *Wall Street Journal*, goop, Home & Family, *Real Simple*, mindbodygreen, NBC, *The Doctors*, and more. When not "dCluttering," she is the proud co-executive director of

OneKid OneWorld, a nonprofit that is building a strong educational foundation for children in impoverished communities throughout Kenya and Central America. She lives in Los Angeles with her partner and their beloved dog, Bodhi.